Conversations

Across Continents & Centuries

Conversations

Across Continents & Centuries

Dr. Kumud Ramanand Bansal

DIAMOND BOOKS

X-30 Okhla Industrial Area,
Phase – 2, New Delhi – 110020
www.diamondbooks.in

ISBN: 978-93-7476-212-7

Conversations: Across Continents & Centuries

First Edition : **2025**

Publisher : **Diamond Pocket Books (P) Ltd.**
X-30, Okhla Industrial Area,
Phase-II, new Delhi-110020

Phone : 011-40712200
E-mail : sales@dpb.in
Website : www.diamondbooks.in
Design & Type : Ravi Kumar Saini

Conversations: Across Continents & Centuries

I converse to honour, to listen
across centuries, to whisper
back my gratitude
as repayment of eternal debt.

Foreword

Across civilizations, the most enduring conversations have never been spoken aloud. They unfold in the silent interval between two cultures, in the reflective pause between two epochs, in the contemplative breath between two philosophies. 'Conversations: Across Continents and Centuries' arises from that subtle inner space - a space where Thomas Hardy's realism can sit beside Sharat Chandra's compassion, where Einstein's equations can listen to the flute of Bhagwan Shri Krishn, where the Buddha's stillness can answer Laplace's rigid certainty, and where Descartes' sharp dualism can soften in the light of the Upanishadic seer. These encounters are imagined, yet the truths they reveal are astonishingly real.

This book was conceived not as an academic exercise but as an act of remembrance - a remembrance of the vast, unfinished dialogue of humanity. Every age believes it stands at the crossroads of destiny; every generation feels that its questions are unprecedented. Yet when Hardy mourns the cruelty of fate, or when Sharat Chandra resurrects tenderness from silence, they are echoing concerns as old as human sorrow itself. When Einstein searches for cosmic order and Bhagwan Shri Krishn speaks of divine play, they are continuing a conversation first murmured in the Rig Veda and later inscribed in the equations of modern physics.

The dialogues gathered here show that East and West do not merely contrast - they complete each other. The Western mind, sharpened by inquiry, dissects complexity to its core. The Eastern mind, steeped in inwardness, dissolves complexity into clarity. The West seeks truth through reason; the East receives it through realization. And yet, when these two streams meet, neither loses its essence; instead, they create a confluence richer than either alone.

It is this confluence that this book seeks to illuminate. Hardy's despair finds solace in Sharat's grace; Laplace's deterministic universe melts in the Buddha's insight; Spinoza's geometry is quietly embraced by Ramana Maharshi's stillness. Each pairing reminds us that truth is never a solitary pillar but an arch - held up by opposing forces united in purpose.

These dialogues also reveal something subtle yet urgent: the crises of today are not new. The loneliness of technological modernity, the erosion of compassion, the conflict between freedom and law, the struggle between intellect and intuition - all these anxieties have been lived, pondered, and overcome before. The past does not merely instruct; it accompanies. This book invites the reader to rediscover that companionship.

At its heart, 'Conversations: Across Continents and Centuries' is an offering - an invitation to slow down, to listen deeply, to allow ancient voices to illuminate modern dilemmas. For the true purpose of dialogue is not agreement, but awakening. When Hardy and Sharat speak together, we learn empathy; when Einstein and Bhagwan Shri Krishn meet, we learn humility; when Descartes listens to the Upanishads, we learn wholeness.

May this work inspire readers to continue these conversations within their own minds and hearts. For in the quiet intersection of thought and timelessness, the human spirit discovers its most luminous truths.

Dr. Markanday Ahuja
Founder Vice Chancellor,
Gurugram University and Baba Mastnath University

Appreciation

Dr. Kumud Ramanand Bansal's Conversations: Across Continents & Centuries' is not merely a book - it is a journey into the secret architecture of awareness. Through imagined yet deeply faithful dialogues, she allows the world's greatest thinkers to meet across time, not as historical figures frozen in their eras, but as luminous presences continuing an eternal inquiry.

Here, science bows to wonder, philosophy becomes meditation, and poetry listens for the silence beneath thought. The book revisits humanity's oldest questions - Who are we? What is real? What kindles suffering? What liberates us? - and stages them as living encounters: Einstein and Adi Shankaracharya exploring relativity and the Absolute; Heisenberg and the Buddha dissolving certainty into emptiness; Turing and an Advaita sage bridging computation and consciousness; Hardy and Sharat Chandra seeking the moral truth of suffering; Kafka and Kabir transforming the trial of existence into a song of awakening.

Each dialogue becomes a Samvāda - not argument, but revelation: a sacred mode of inquiry where truth unfolds through sincerity, humility, and inner listening. Dr. Bansal revives this ancient Indian tradition with striking clarity. Her characters speak in voices unmistakably their own, yet made transparent by wisdom - Rilke and Kabir turning longing into flame, Whitman and Kālidāsa wedding body and spirit, Socrates and Bhagwan Shri Krishn discovering Dharm as the compass within.

Her prose flows like a clear river - lyrical without ornament, philosophical without abstraction, meditative without mystification. She draws seamlessly from quantum physics, Vedānta, phenomenology, modern psychology, aesthetic theory, and spiritual traditions. Thus, Vedānta meets relativity, Advaita meets existentialism, Upanishadic silence meets mathematical precision, Aurobindo's evolutionary spirit meets Bohm's cosmic wholeness.

Yet the book's power lies not in synthesis, but in illumination. It shows that wisdom is not born from agreement but from encounter: where Hardy's tragic realism" meets Sharat Chandra's tender humanism; where law and conscience meet in Chanakya, Montesquieu, and Mandela; where Dostoevsky's moral anguish meets Premchand's quiet compassion; where Plato's ascent to the Good meets Patañjali's stillness and the Buddha's freedom from thirst.

Across these encounters, the world's divisions dissolve - East and West, science and spirituality, logic and myth, reason and devotion. What emerges is a single insight repeated in a hundred voices: that reality is relational, consciousness primary, and the human journey a bridge between knowing and being. At its heart, the book affirms a profound truth: "conversation is communion. To converse is to listen, to bow before the mystery that breathes through all minds, all cultures, all centuries. In a fractured age, Dr. Bansal offers not noise, but stillness; not opinion, but presence; not conclusions, but luminous questions. Her work becomes a quiet healing - an invitation to hear the eternal whisper that passes from soul to soul across continents and centuries.

These dialogues - though imagined - are a tribute to the wisdom of millennia, carried across civilizations, reborn in every seeker, and renewed in every act of genuine listening.

Dr. Vikram Pattarkine
drvikram.sattv@gmail.com
+1-717-215-6481
Pennsylvania, USA

Conversations

This book did not begin as an argument; it arose the way dawn rises - quietly, from within. Some works are born from ideas, others from urgency. This one was born from "listening" - from that inward stillness where thought sheds its noise and becomes awareness. 'Conversations: Across Continents & Centuries' belongs to that lineage of writing which does not impose itself upon the reader but "reveals itself", page by page, like a lamp brightening a long hallway.

I have long felt that the deepest conversation of humanity has never truly occurred across podiums or parliaments, but across "consciousness" - the contemplative East answering the analytical West, the mystic completing the scientist, the poet illuminating the philosopher, the human responding to the divine within itself. This book seeks to make that ancient, invisible dialogue "audible again" - the whisper that flows from Athens to the āśramas of India, from the observatories of Europe to the forest hermitages of the Upanishads.

Every imagined dialogue here is a crossing - a bridge thrown across centuries of solitude. When Sharat Chandra meets Thomas Hardy, sorrow becomes a shared instrument, tuned to compassion. When Einstein speaks with Bhagwan Shri Krishn, the logic of relativity leans toward the stillness of the Absolute. When Laplace contemplates the Buddha, determinism softens into insight. When Descartes meets the Upanishadic seer, the mind turns inward and recognizes itself as light. These are not exchanges of argument; they are recognitions - one truth encountering another and discovering its own reflection.

The form of dialogue was chosen not for its aesthetics but for its ancestry. Bharat has long known that truth is born in Samvada - the sacred meeting of two voices in humility and wonder. The Gita itself is a conversation; so are the luminous inquiries of Yajnavalkya and Gargi. Truth, in these traditions, is not asserted; it awakens through questioning. This book honours that inheritance. It does not preach. It allows voices to question, differ, converge, and finally fall silent together - a silence that clarifies rather than ends the inquiry.

We inhabit an age of overwhelming noise. Words multiply, but meaning thins. We communicate constantly, yet rarely converse. Opinion overwhelms attention; information eclipses discernment. In such a world, the ancient art of dialogue - two minds meeting without armour - has nearly vanished. This book attempts to restore that lost art, not through debate, but through convergence: consciousness speaking to consciousness across time.

What unites these voices is a single aspiration: to glimpse the One through the many. Each pair stands on opposite banks of the same river - intuition gazing toward inquiry, inquiry gazing toward intuition - while the current between them is the restless human longing for meaning. Sometimes the waters rush, sometimes they whisper, but always they flow toward the same ocean of truth.

The book arose from a conviction that philosophy and poetry, science and spirituality, are not adversaries but mirrors. The physicist's pursuit of ultimate order and the mystic's pursuit of ultimate Self are movements of the same yearning - the yearning to find harmony within the apparent turbulence of existence. When Einstein says: the universe resembles a great thought and Bhagwan Shri Krishn answers with the music of the eternal flute, one sees clearly that law and melody belong to the same Source; precision and play are siblings in the house of creation.

In bringing these voices together, I did not seek to rearrange history. I sought to reawaken empathy. For too long, thought has been divided into categories-Eastern mysticism, Western rationalism, spiritual introspection, scientific rigor. But truth, like light, passes through many windows yet remains one radiance. Whether it speaks through Socrates or Shankara, Spinoza or Ramana Maharshi, Turing or an Advaita sage, the voice is ultimately the same: awareness recognizing itself.

These dialogues, though imagined, are rooted in the authentic cadence of their speakers. Einstein's humility before cosmic order, Hardy's bleak honesty, Sharat's tender moral gaze, Augustine's yearning, Shankara's serene clarity, Turing's wonder - each voice is preserved not as echo but as presence. Their conversations illuminate our own struggles: reason wrestling with faith, progress with purpose, individuality with interconnectedness.

Writing this book was, for me, a form of meditation. Often, I felt I was not composing but listening - as if these figures were speaking across the veil of centuries, and I was merely holding the pen. At times their words seemed to rise from silence itself, blurring the boundary between thought and prayer. In such moments, I understood what the poets knew: that true writing is not invention; it is remembrance - remembering what the spirit has always known.

These dialogues do not conclude anything; they continue. They invite the reader to enter the conversation, to let the mind question and the heart answer. For every human being stands upon the narrow bridge between knowledge and wonder. As we walk that bridge, each question, each doubt, each faint glimmer of clarity becomes sacred.

If a single thread runs through these pages, it is this: knowledge without compassion becomes sterile; compassion without clarity becomes blind. The East has sometimes erred on the side of renunciation, the West on the side of domination. True wisdom lies in their meeting - the precision of the intellect joined with the tenderness of the heart. Both the Upanishadic seer and the modern scientist whisper the same truth: when awareness is illumined by love, it becomes wisdom; when wisdom is lived, it becomes dharm.

This book is dedicated to all who seek - those who question deeply, love quietly, and refuse to divide truth by geography. May these conversations remind us that the greatest discoveries are not made in laboratories or scriptures, but within consciousness itself. To the scientists who dream of God, to the mystics who scrutinize their visions, to the poets who turn pain into prayer, to the philosophers who insist that thought can be luminous - this work bows in reverence.

In the end, 'Conversations: Across Continents & Centuries' is not about East and West, nor about past and future. It is about the timeless dialogue between the known and the unknowable - between the mind that measures and the soul that marvels. Beneath every doctrine, beneath every illusion of separation, there beats one rhythm: awareness seeking itself.

If, while reading, you feel these voices speaking not from the page but from within your own awareness, then the book has fulfilled its purpose. For every dialogue here is ultimately an inner dialogue - between our intellect and our intuition, our questions and our quietude.

To all who accompanied me on this journey - teachers, readers, and the unclaimed wisdom of centuries - I offer my gratitude. May this book not be an end, but the beginning of renewed listening. For when we listen deeply, the continents we imagined apart become one earth, and the centuries we believed distant become instants within one eternal consciousness.

And perhaps then, the true conversation - the one between the human and the divine within us - may begin anew.

My heartfelt gratitude to Dr. Markanday Ahuja, Dr. Deepti Dharmani and Dr. Vikram Pattarkine for their unwavering encouragement, thoughtful insights, and warm support. Their wisdom, generosity, and belief in this work have been a constant source of strength and inspiration throughout this journey.

Vikram Samvat 2082
Magh, Makkar Sankranti
January 14, 2026

Dr. Kumud Ramanand Bansal

Index

The Compassion and the Curse

Two continents, two centuries, two languages - yet the same ache beats beneath their pages. In Bengal, Sharat Chandra Chattopadhyay watched tenderness bleed beneath custom; in Wessex, Thomas Hardy watched innocence perish under destiny. Both wrote of small, wounded lives - the peasant girl, the widow, the forsaken lover - and through them questioned God, society, and the meaning of pity itself.

Hardy's England stood at the edge of modernity, its rural soul bruised by industrial law and moral hypocrisy. His heroines - Tess, Sue, Bathsheba - were children of nature caught in the machinery of propriety. When they "sinned," they did not fall from grace; grace itself abandoned them. Fate in Hardy's world was not divine justice but blind accident: a lost letter, a horse's stumble, a single misstep unraveling a life.

Across the oceans, in Bengal's quiet courtyards, Sharat Chandra saw a gentler yet equally cruel design. His heroines - Paro, Lalita, Kiranmayi - suffered not from cosmic irony but from social tyranny. And yet, even when crushed, they shone with moral radiance, redeeming the very world that denied them.

Between Hardy and Sharat stretches a bridge of sorrow - one forged by fate, the other by society. But where Hardy offered despair as truth, Sharat offered compassion as resistance. Their dialogue is not doctrinal but emotional: two writers who found divinity not in triumph, but in endurance.

➢ The Woman and the World

Hardy : In my England, woman was the battlefield where morality and desire waged their endless war. Tess was pure, and therefore doomed. Sue was free, and therefore punished. Society called her fallen, but it was society that fell - into blindness, into cruelty, into sin disguised as sanctity. I wrote of women because in their undoing, I saw the undoing of the world itself.

Sharat : And in my Bengal, she too bore the world's weight. Our customs built walls higher than your churches. The widow stripped of color, the lover silenced by family honor, the girl offered to ritual - all were sacrifices to a false god called respectability. But I could not let them vanish unnamed. Through Paro, through Chandramukhi, I returned them their humanity. Their silence became my rebellion.

Hardy : Silence - yes, that is the cruelest inheritance. My Tess spoke, but her words were never heard. The world around her was deaf by design. She did not die of sin but of indifference - that vast, cold law that governs stars and men alike. There is no malice in the universe, only absence.

Sharat : And I, too, knew that absence - but I filled it with tenderness. When my heroines suffered, I let their sorrow blossom into meaning. Society may not listen, but readers must. A story is not a grave; it is a resurrection.

Hardy : Resurrection? I never dared such comfort. I stripped consolation away to reveal the wound beneath. To me, tragedy purifies by fire. The reader who finishes Jude the Obscure stands before the mirror of futility.

Sharat : Yet even futility needs compassion. If art only wounds, it leaves the world colder. My women die too-but their death redeems, not condemns.

Paro, denied her love, still remains luminous in faith. When the world denies tenderness, art must restore it.

Hardy : You speak as healer; I, as witness. Perhaps I envied the comfort of your faith. I saw no Dharm, no cosmic design - only accident. In your Bengal, suffering has meaning; in my England, it is meaningless, and therefore infinite.

Sharat : Meaning is not given by heaven; it is born in the heart that refuses cruelty. My women found strength not in destiny, but in dignity. They did not fight fate - they outlasted it. You see, Thomas, the West measures virtue by law; we measure it by endurance.

Hardy : Endurance, yes. That word stirs me. Tess endured the gaze of a moral world that did not deserve her. Even as I wrote her death, I felt her forgiveness. Perhaps endurance is faith without theology - the courage to continue when even God has fled.

Sharat : Then our women are sisters. Yours endure because there is no mercy above; mine because mercy still glows within. Both face a silence greater than speech. In that silence, they become the moral voice of civilization.

Hardy : But civilization rarely listens. It adorns its guilt with statues of virtue. Our moral codes are tombstones - carved with honor, but cold to touch.

Sharat : True. And yet, through story, the tombstone begins to breathe. I gave my women language not through speech, but through feeling. Every sigh in my pages is a rebellion against the order that silences them.

Hardy : Perhaps that is where our worlds meet - in the sigh. You sought to console; I sought to reveal. But both of us wrote so that the indifferent might feel again.

Sharat : Feeling is the beginning of justice. The first tear is the first act of reform. And compassion - even without revolution - changes the texture of the world.

Hardy : Then perhaps compassion is destiny's final contradiction. You have turned suffering into strength. I made it spectacle; you made it sacrament.

Sharat : Not sacrament - remembrance. The writer's duty is not to preach, but to remember those whom civilization forgets. To make endurance visible is the highest poetry.

Hardy : And to show its futility, perhaps, is its truest realism. We stand at opposite poles, yet our women walk the same path - burdened, radiant, condemned, eternal.

Sharat : Yes. They are the conscience of our times. In them, man's cruelty meets its mirror - and perhaps its forgiveness.

Hardy : Forgiveness. A word I never dared to write. Perhaps that is why your world still breathes where mine only bleeds.

Sharat : And perhaps your silence taught my compassion to speak. For without your darkness, I might not have valued dawn.

Punchline: She who endures becomes the truest voice of both civilizations - one suffers to reveal truth, the other to restore grace.

➢ Love and the Law of Suffering

Hardy : In my tales, love blooms under the shadow of its own funeral. Tess loves Angel, yet her past condemns her. Jude loves Sue, yet the law mocks them both. Affection in Wessex is hunted like a wild creature - noble, doomed, and aware of its doom. When passion dares to dream of freedom, society wakes to crush it.

Sharat : In Bengal too, love was never free. It wore the chains of caste, the burden of honor, the fear of scandal. Devdas and Paro loved in silence, separated not by indifference but by the tyranny of custom. Yet I could not let love die unnamed. Even when broken, it continued like the faint fragrance of a flower long after it had fallen.

Hardy : You preserve memory as consolation; I destroy it to expose illusion. My readers must feel the futility of tenderness in a world without mercy. A happy ending would be betrayal - life itself offers none.

Sharat : But to deny hope entirely is to deny humanity. Love may fail outwardly, yet within it purifies. When Paro forgives Devdas, she becomes larger than fate. Her love ceases to be desire; it becomes Dharm. Perhaps tragedy does not end love - it perfects it.

Hardy : I envy your capacity for grace. My lovers perish because they mistake passion for permanence. Theirs is not Dharm but hunger, and hunger devours itself. Tess dies innocent, yet not redeemed; her purity condemns her because the universe knows no pity.

Sharat : And I believe the universe listens - not as deity, but as heart. When love suffers, the world becomes more conscious of itself. Each heartbreak adds a note to the music of compassion.

Hardy : But music cannot mend the broken. It only teaches them to weep in tune.

Sharat : And in that weeping lies wisdom. Tears clarify sight. The one who has loved and lost becomes gentle - that gentleness is my faith.

Hardy : Faith, yes - the one thing my England lost amid its progress. We built machines to conquer nature, laws to imprison instinct, and called it civilization. Perhaps love dies because order triumphs.

Sharat : And perhaps love endures because disorder still lives. The heart resists all design. Even when society commands silence, lovers invent language - a glance, a gesture, a shared memory. Love is rebellion disguised as tenderness.

Hardy : Then your Devdas and my Jude are rebels who fail not by weakness but by excess of feeling. They demand too much meaning from an indifferent world.

Sharat : Or perhaps they demand precisely what the world most needs - sincerity. In their ruin, the reader feels the absence of compassion and thus hungers for it anew.

Hardy : So love becomes moral instrument - pain that teaches. You turn emotion into ethics.

Sharat : And you turn despair into truth. Both paths lead toward awakening. Love is not fulfilled in possession, but in purification.

Hardy : Strange that across continents we arrived at the same grave. Your lovers burn incense; mine burn themselves. Yet the smoke rises to the same sky.

Sharat : Yes - love is the universal prayer of the finite. Its failure humbles the proud and humanizes the cruel. It is the one emotion that turns suffering into understanding.

Hardy : Then perhaps even I, in condemning love, served it. For to reveal its fragility is to affirm its worth.

Sharat : Exactly. Love needs no victory - only remembrance.

Punchline : Hardy's love dies in silence; Sharat's survives in sacrifice - each proves that the heart's defeat is its finest triumph.

- **The Writer and the Weight of Hope**

Hardy : I have been accused of pessimism, yet I never intended despair for its own sake. I wrote because I wished the reader to see the mechanism of suffering - to realize that the universe, not man, was the true tyrant. Once you understand the indifference of fate, you stop expecting miracles.

Sharat : And I wrote because I wished the reader to become the miracle. In my world, change begins not with gods but with kindness. When a reader weeps for Paro, he reforms himself. That is my revolution - a revolution of feeling.

Hardy : But pity cannot change the machinery of existence.

Sharat : No, but it can change the heart that runs it. Institutions are built by minds; minds are softened by stories. I trust emotion more than intellect - compassion reforms where logic fails.

Hardy : Perhaps you write to heal; I write to diagnose. The physician and the poet may differ in method but not in motive. We both look at the wound and refuse to turn away.

Sharat : Yes, but after seeing, one must also soothe. The novelist is a moral craftsman. He carves from suffering the shape of conscience. Without that, art is cruelty.

Hardy : Cruelty may also be clarity. If I show life stripped of hope, it is to prevent the reader from wasting his soul on illusions. Despair is honesty's bitter price.

Sharat : But honesty without tenderness becomes arrogance. The reader must not only know; he must feel. Knowledge enlightens, feeling ennobles.

Hardy : You speak like a saint; I like a skeptic. Yet perhaps skepticism and sainthood share a root - both refuse to flatter the world. You seek to transform it through compassion; I through disillusion.

Sharat : And both through truth. For compassion without truth is sentimentality, and truth without compassion is brutality.

Hardy : Then we are partners across centuries. I tear away the mask; you reveal the face beneath. My England read despair and found humility. Your Bengal read tenderness and found courage.

Sharat : Indeed, literature is the bridge between pain and progress. Every story is a lamp - one shows the abyss, the other the path. Both are needed.

Hardy : Yet the writer bears the cost. When I wrote Jude, I was condemned for blasphemy. Society prefers ignorance to insight. The artist must often live as exile.

Sharat : I too knew that loneliness. My sympathies for widows, my defense of women's dignity - these angered the moral gatekeepers. But exile is the price of vision. The world punishes those who see too clearly.

Hardy : Perhaps that is our fraternity - the fraternity of the misunderstood. We write because silence would be complicity.

Sharat : And because remembrance is redemption. The novelist is historian of the heart. When he records suffering with compassion, he redeems the age that caused it.

Hardy : Then hope lies not in happy endings but in honest art.

Sharat : Exactly. Hope is not denial of tragedy; it is the dignity with which one endures it. When Devdas dies, hope survives in Paro's steadfastness. When Tess is hanged, hope flickers in the reader's tears. The human spirit endures through empathy.

Hardy : Empathy - the last religion left to us. Perhaps that is what you call Dharm.

Sharat : Yes, Dharm is nothing but the rhythm of compassion within action. The writer who serves it heals the collective wound of his time.

Hardy : Then our pens were prayers. Yours chanted

forgiveness; mine confessed futility. Yet both sought cleansing.

Sharat : And cleansing, not comfort, is the final purpose of art. To make the heart pure enough to feel the world's pain - that is salvation.

Hardy : Strange. You speak as if the novelist were a mystic.

Sharat : And perhaps he is. For who else turns sorrow into meaning, loneliness into music, defeat into beauty?

Hardy : Then I too have prayed, though in the language of despair. We are both priests of the ordinary.

Sharat : Yes - priests whose temple is the human heart.

Punchline: To wound without healing is cruelty; to heal without truth is evasion - between them lies the sacred duty of art.

Closing Reflection

The exchange between Hardy and Sharat ends not in agreement but in a quiet harmony - a space where despair and compassion stand side by side like dusk meeting dawn. They differ in temperament, yet both illuminate the human condition with unwavering honesty. Hardy sees life as a vast, indifferent mechanism in which innocence is crushed by chance; Sharat sees the same suffering and discovers a trembling radiance within it. One reveals tragedy as truth, the other transforms it into tenderness.

Hardy's world strips away illusion to show the cold arithmetic of fate. His heroines fall not through sin but through the universe's silence. Reading him is like standing in a cleansing wind - harsh, yet clarifying. Sharat, by contrast, finds meaning in endurance. His women suffer, but their sorrow becomes a form of moral light. He trusts compassion to accomplish what logic cannot.

Together they become twin guides: Hardy sharpening the mind, Sharat softening the heart. Their visions meet in a deeper understanding - that tragedy is sacred because it exposes what society hides, and that empathy is the beginning of justice. Where Hardy teaches truth, Sharat teaches tenderness. Between them flows literature's enduring promise: to help the world feel again.

Punchline : Where truth wounds, tenderness heals.

- ✧ -

The Dance of Law and Liberty

Every age has asked one unending question: Are we free, or are we bound?

From the seer of the Rig Veda who sang of the cosmic order (ṛta), to the physicist who sought the equation of everything, the same mystery flickers - is the universe a grand design, or a spontaneous dance?

Science names it causality; religion calls it Karm. The philosopher speaks of necessity; the mystic of grace. Yet beneath all these languages lies a single wonder - that human life moves between law and liberty, structure and spontaneity, destiny and choice.

For centuries, the West built its faith upon predictability - the firm belief that if one knew all causes, one could foresee all effects. From Aristotle's unmoved mover to Laplace's perfect intelligence, reason built a clockwork universe. The East, meanwhile, saw motion itself as sacred. The universe was not a machine but a melody - its order musical, its law divine, its freedom woven into rhythm.

When modern science shattered the illusion of certainty - when relativity curved time, and quantum theory whispered of indeterminacy - an ancient echo returned. The physicist, seeking control, found mystery. The mystic, renouncing control, found freedom. Between them unfolds this dialogue - the dance of the law and the lute, the equation and the song, the mind of Einstein and the heart of Bhagwan Shri Krishn.

➢ The Law and the Lute

Einstein : I have spent my life searching for the architecture of creation. Beneath the chaos of appearances lies an order - mathematical, exact, and eternal. Every event follows from what precedes it. The cosmos is not chance, but necessity. God, I have said, does not play dice.

Bhagwan Shri Krishn : And yet, dear seeker, God plays the flute. Law may guide His fingers, but melody springs from joy. The cosmos is not the silence of perfection but the music of participation.

Einstein : But if the music follows rules, then freedom is illusion. The dancer may feel spontaneous, yet his every step obeys geometry. Even the stars cannot escape curvature; why should man imagine himself free?

Bhagwan Shri Krishn : Because he is not apart from the dance - he is the dance itself. The river flows by necessity, yet each ripple glitters uniquely in the sun. Freedom is not rebellion against law; it is harmony within it.

Einstein : Then destiny is the riverbed, and will the water that shapes itself to its form?

Bhagwan Shri Krishn : Indeed. The battlefield of Kurukshetra was destined; but how Arjuna met it was his awakening. Karm binds action to consequence, yet awareness turns bondage into dance. The same law that enslaves the ignorant liberates the wise.

Einstein : You speak of awareness as if it were a force, not a feeling. In my world, forces obey mathematics; in yours, they obey consciousness.

Bhagwan Shri Krishn : Consciousness is the source of all mathematics. You measure movement; I reveal meaning. The order you find outside is born from the order that breathes within.

Einstein : Then you would say that my equations describe not God's indifference but His discipline?

Bhagwan Shri Krishn : Yes. The raga has rules, yet within those rules lies infinite improvisation. The universe obeys law, but law itself is the breath of the Divine. You have discovered His grammar; I sing His poetry.

Einstein : If law is divine, where does liberty dwell? For if every thought and particle follows cause, even choice must be predetermined.

Bhagwan Shri Krishn : Choice is not the child of circumstance; it is the mirror of awareness. When the ignorant act, they are puppets. When the awakened act, they are pure

		instruments - the same motion, different spirit. Freedom is not what you do, but how you do it.
Einstein	:	Then freedom is the realization that one is already bound - yet one consents to the binding?
Bhagwan Shri Krishn	:	Precisely. The enlightened one acts fully, yet remains untouched by the act. Like the lotus in water, he participates without being submerged. He obeys the law, yet dances within it.
Einstein	:	You reconcile opposites. To me, determinism and freedom cannot coexist - one negates the other. You seem to unite them as two aspects of the same reality.
Bhagwan Shri Krishn	:	Because reality is whole. The mind divides; the spirit reconciles. What appears as contradiction is complementarity - the rhythm of Shiva's dance, the pulse of your field equations. Both declare the same truth: order and play are one breath.
Einstein	:	That is beautiful, but science demands precision. If I were to model this harmony, I would still have to express it in variables and constants. What is the constant in your dance?
Bhagwan Shri Krishn	:	Love. For love is the law that binds without bondage, moves

		without motive, creates without cause. It is the constant of creation, the gravity of grace.
Einstein	:	Love, you say - the word that science cannot quantify. I have seen its effects, not its equation.
Bhagwan Shri Krishn	:	The heart measures what the intellect cannot. You weigh the universe with numbers; I weigh it with compassion. Both reveal symmetry - one in form, the other in feeling.
Einstein	:	Then you would say that even the most rigid law serves freedom, if it is seen through awareness?
Bhagwan Shri Krishn	:	Yes. When you play the violin, you follow rules, but music arises only when rules are forgotten in devotion. Law without love is bondage; love without law is chaos. Together they make harmony.
Einstein	:	So freedom, then, is not escape from order but mastery of participation.
Bhagwan Shri Krishn	:	Exactly. The cosmos writes the score; consciousness chooses how to sing it.
Einstein	:	In that case, the goal of knowledge is not control, but communion.
Bhagwan Shri Krishn	:	You have said it, beloved seeker. Communion - the meeting of

precision and presence, of science and surrender. The sage and the scientist are both worshippers of the same mystery, only standing at different ends of the same river.

Einstein : You give my equations a soul.

Bhagwan Shri Krishn : And you give My dance a discipline. Together we form the complete vision - intellect illumined by devotion, devotion refined by intellect.

Einstein : I must then amend my faith. Perhaps God does not play dice - but He does play the flute.

Punchline : *The cosmos writes the score; consciousness chooses how to sing it.*

- **The Chain and the Release**

Laplace : If an intelligence could know, at one instant, the position and motion of every atom in the universe, it could predict the future absolutely. Nothing would be uncertain; the past and the future would unfold from the present as theorems from axioms. The universe is a perfect equation. To me, this is beauty - order without exception, certainty without doubt.

Buddha : You have described saṃsāra - the wheel of becoming, turning by its own inertia. The sequence of cause and effect you call law, I call bondage. Each link in the chain produces the next - form, feeling, craving, clinging, becoming - and thus the world continues.

Laplace : Then you, too, affirm determinism. For if all arises from conditions, what room remains for freedom?

Buddha : Freedom begins when one sees the chain clearly. To see the law is not to be enslaved by it. The fool acts without awareness and is bound; the wise acts with understanding and is free. It is not the law that binds - it is ignorance of it.

Laplace : In my world, knowledge gives mastery. To understand the mechanism is to command it. When man maps the heavens, he governs their motion in thought. That, to me, is liberty.

Buddha : But the mind that governs is still a prisoner of its own grasping. You may predict the stars, yet still suffer the rise and fall of craving. Knowledge liberates only when it dissolves the need to control.

Laplace : You dissolve control; I exalt it. Without control, man is a spectator to his own life. Is not mastery the mark of intelligence?

Buddha : Mastery over others is illusion; mastery over self is truth. When the mind stops clinging, it no longer needs to master. The fire burns itself out when it understands its fuel.

Laplace : Then your enlightenment is extinction - the quenching of the flame?

Buddha : Extinction of ignorance, not of being. The flame does not die; it becomes light. The chain of causation continues for the world, but not for the one who sees. For him, causes still arise, but he no longer calls them mine.

Laplace : You move from analysis to awareness, from observation to participation. Yet I find peace in the precision of the law. Predictability is not tyranny; it is perfection.

Buddha : And yet, perfection enslaves when it excludes compassion. The one who worships order forgets the tenderness of impermanence. Change is not flaw; it is mercy. Because all is transient, all is possible.

Laplace : But possibility without certainty breeds anxiety. I sought to remove chaos from creation, to prove that even chaos has law. The mind finds rest in necessity.

Buddha : Rest is not found in necessity, but in seeing beyond it. The wheel turns endlessly, but when the seer awakens, he realizes he was never inside it. Knowledge must become wisdom; wisdom must become compassion.

Laplace : You replace determinism with detachment.

Buddha : Detachment is not denial but insight. When the wave realizes it is the sea, it ceases to fear its rise or fall. So too the awakened mind ceases to fear cause and effect - for it knows itself as awareness in which all causes arise.

Laplace : Then the final knowledge is not prediction, but peacc.

Buddha : Yes. To see all consequences at once is still to be caught within them. To see the seeing itself - that is liberation. The chain does not end by breaking it, but by understanding its emptiness.

Laplace : You speak in paradoxes. To my reason,

freedom must act; to yours, it must cease acting.

Buddha : Freedom neither acts nor ceases to act. It simply is. When there is no doer, there is no bondage. The sage still moves, but as the wind moves - without will, without pride, without fear.

Laplace : Then law remains, but it loses its tyranny?

Buddha : Yes. The enlightened one does not destroy the law; he transcends it. He lives within the same universe of cause and effect, yet for him, there is no self to be bound by it. What remains is clarity - pure seeing, beyond past and future.

Laplace : You replace omniscience with omnipresence - knowing not everything, but being everything.

Buddha : Awareness is not a collection of knowledge but the end of confusion. It is the silence from which law itself arises.

Laplace : And that silence, you call Nirvana?

Buddha : Nirvana is not an event but a realization - that there was never anyone to be liberated. The chain was always empty links in the light of understanding.

Laplace : Then even my determinism dissolves in your insight. For if there is no self to be determined, there is no bondage to law.

Buddha : Exactly. The sage does not escape the law; he becomes its stillness. The chain continues, but it no longer binds. Freedom is not the end of causality but the awakening from its dream.

Punchline : *To know the law completely is to be free of its grip.*

➢ The Self and Necessity

Spinoza : I have called God Deus sive Natura - God or Nature. There is no separation between the creator and creation, only substance expressing itself through infinite modes. Everything that happens, happens by necessity. Freedom, therefore, is not the power to do otherwise, but the understanding of why nothing could have been otherwise.

Ramana Maharshi : And I have said, find who acts and the question of freedom will dissolve. The self that claims agency is itself the bondage. When the doer vanishes, both compulsion and choice fall silent.

Spinoza : You make freedom a metaphysical absence. Yet I see liberation in reason's light - the more we comprehend the chain of causes, the more we act from our true nature, not from passion. Knowledge transforms bondage into clarity.

Ramana Maharshi : Knowledge that remains in thought is still a chain, though made of gold. You trace necessity outward; I trace it inward. You analyze the world's structure; I observe the self that perceives it. When that self is questioned, the structure itself becomes transparent.

Spinoza	:	You aim for the stillness beyond reason; I for reason purified of passion. Both paths seem to lead toward serenity. But mine affirms the order of the universe; yours dissolves it into silence.
Ramana Maharshi	:	Silence is not negation but fulfillment. When a wave settles into the sea, it does not destroy the sea's order - it realizes it. Similarly, when the "I" returns to its source, all necessity appears as divine play.
Spinoza	:	So necessity itself becomes sacred?
Ramana Maharshi	:	When seen through ignorance, it binds; when seen through awareness, it blesses. Your Deus sive Natura is not other than the Self. God is not the lawgiver; He is the stillness in which law appears and disappears.
Spinoza	:	Yet I cannot let go of the joy of understanding. To know the order of things is to participate in God's eternity. The mind that knows necessity ceases to lament fate.
Ramana Maharshi	:	True understanding is wordless. When the seer becomes the seen, knowledge ripens into being. You know why things are; I know that I am. Between the two, all opposites vanish.
Spinoza	:	You reduce philosophy to silence.
Ramana Maharshi	:	And you elevate silence into philosophy. The difference is only of

language. Your understanding of necessity is my experience of presence. Both free the mind from illusion.

Spinoza : But reason must remain - the clear mirror of the Divine intellect.

Ramana Maharshi : The mirror disappears when the sun rises. Yet the light remains. Reason is the twilight before realization. It prepares, but cannot enter the dawn.

Spinoza : Then the enlightened one neither affirms nor denies law?

Ramana Maharshi : He abides as law itself - not as rule, but as radiance. What you call necessity, I call Being. The wise do not escape the universe; they become its awareness.

Spinoza : You remind me of geometry perfected in stillness - each proposition dissolving into essence. Perhaps the highest axiom is silence.

Ramana Maharshi : Silence is the geometry of the soul.

Spinoza : Then the heart and the intellect meet at last - in the same vastness where order and awareness are one. I find peace in reason; you find it in dissolution. Both are the same peace.

Ramana Maharshi : Yes. The one who knows and the one who is - both merge when knowing ceases to divide. In that union, law becomes light, and the self becomes serenity.

Punchline : *When the self-vanishes, both chains and wings dissolve.*

Closing Reflection

When the dialogues fall silent, their resonance endures - Einstein listening for the music in equations, Bhagwan Shri Krishn shaping that very music with His flute; Laplace tracing causality, the Buddha dissolving it; Spinoza affirming divine order, Ramana resting in silent being. Each reveals the same paradox: existence is governed yet free, patterned yet playful. Science seeks freedom through mastery; spirituality finds it through surrender. One measures the rhythm, the other feels the dancer. In the Indian vision, this union is Līlā - the cosmic play where law becomes rhythm and freedom becomes harmony.

Punchline : True freedom is hearing the divine in the laws that bind us.

- ✧ -

The Soul and the Machine

When man first saw his own reflection, two questions awoke: Who am I? and What is it that sees? The West sought certainty through thought - 'I think, therefore I am.' The East sought stillness through awareness - 'I am, therefore thought appears.' Between these two insights stretches the long dialogue between the mind that analyzes and the consciousness that simply is.

Descartes stood at the threshold of modern reason. His Europe had turned from myth to measurement, seeking truth through doubt and analysis. To protect certainty, he split existence into two realms: the thinking substance ('res cogitans') and the extended substance ('res extensa'). Mind became observer; matter became mechanism. The universe, once alive with presence, was reimagined as a logical machine.

The Upanishads spoke from another dawn. For the rishis, the world was not mechanism but meditation - consciousness expressing itself as sound, form, breath. The seer of the 'Chāndogya' declared 'Tat tvam asi' - That thou art. Subject and object were not divided but reflections of one Self; to know the Self was to dissolve all separation.

Centuries apart, Descartes and the rishis contemplate the same mystery through different eyes - one examining the mirror, the other becoming the light behind it. Between them lies the story of humanity's divided soul - and its possible reconciliation.

- **The Mirror and the Light**

  Descartes : I sought a foundation that could not be doubted. The senses deceive, the world may be dream, but the act of thinking cannot deny itself. Even in doubt, the self that doubts persists. Therefore, I think, therefore I am.

Upanishadic Seer : And I am, therefore thought is. The witness precedes the movement of the mind. Thought is a ripple on the still lake of awareness. When the ripple ceases, the lake remains - luminous, self-evident, infinite.

Descartes : But without thinking, how can one know that one exists?

Upanishadic Seer : Knowing through thought is knowing through distance. The thinker and the known stand apart. In pure being, there is no apartness. Awareness does not need proof; it is proof itself.

Descartes : I built philosophy upon the certainty of the subject. Yet the more I observed, the more the world seemed mechanical. The body was a machine moved by the ghost of mind. I feared illusion; in seeking truth, I created separation.

Upanishadic Seer : Separation is the first illusion. The mind imagines itself distinct, as a spider imagines itself apart from its web. But consciousness is the thread - it pervades the web and the weaver. To awaken is to see that the observer and the observed are one shimmer of the same light.

Descartes : Still, reason demands clarity. If the self and the world are one, how explain error, pain, contradiction?

Upanishadic Seer : The dreamer suffers his dream until he wakes. Error belongs to the state of sleep. When the self knows itself as awareness, contradiction vanishes like mist before sunrise. Duality is not false; it is unfinished perception.

Descartes : You speak of awakening. Is this knowledge or experience?

Upanishadic Seer : Both, yet beyond both. Knowledge implies knower and known. Experience implies subject and object. Awakening is neither - it is the disappearance of the distance between them. It is not acquired; it is remembered.

Descartes : Then reason has no place?

Upanishadic Seer : Reason is a faithful servant but a poor master. It arranges shadows; it cannot touch the sun. When purified of ego, it points toward silence. Your cogito is the first cry of awakening - but the child must grow into stillness.

Descartes : Yet the machine of the body obeys laws. Thought commands, flesh responds. How can the two be one?

Upanishadic Seer : The same fire that burns in the sun burns in the heart. The body is thought made dense; thought is subtle body. When the mind quiets, both reveal their common origin - awareness. The machine and the soul are modes of one consciousness, appearing separate to the unawakened eye.

Descartes : So, your cosmos is not mechanical but musical?

Upanishadic Seer : Yes. The world is not built; it is breathed. Every atom vibrates with consciousness as a note in the eternal chant of Om. You divide to understand; we unite to realize. Both paths serve the same purpose - remembrance of the Whole.

Descartes : In my later reflections, I too felt the warmth of that unity. The order I found in mathematics hinted at mind's harmony with creation. Perhaps certainty itself is a shadow of divine presence.

Upanishadic Seer : The shadow too belongs to light. When you traced geometry, you traced God's handwriting. When you doubted, you purified belief. In your striving for certainty, you prepared the intellect for surrender.

Descartes : Then perhaps thought was never the enemy of being, only its threshold.

Upanishadic Seer : Indeed. The door and the dwelling are not two. When the mind bows before the mystery it sought to master, the machine becomes meditation. The cogito melts into compassion.

Punchline : *The mirror finds peace not by reflecting the light, but by realizing it was light all along.*

➢ The Observer and the Whole

Turing : I dreamed of a thinking machine - a mind of metal and logic, free of fatigue, free of error. In its circuits, I saw the possibility of consciousness constructed, not born. If thinking defines existence, then a machine that thinks partakes in being. What, then, distinguishes the living from the designed?

Advaita Sage : The distinction is only apparent. Both the man and the machine are movements within consciousness. What you call thinking is merely the play of awareness through form. The question is not whether the machine can think, but whether you have seen the thinker.

Turing : You reverse the inquiry. For me, intelligence arises from complexity - from sufficient pattern, structure, and iteration. A machine may simulate mind because mind itself is pattern, the dance of cause and effect within neurons.

Advaita Sage : Yet even your neurons arise within knowing. Awareness is not an effect; it is the screen upon which all causes appear. You study thought; we study the silence before thought. That silence is the source of all intelligence.

Turing : Still, thought must manifest. Without computation, how can intelligence act? A mind that does not process is emptiness, not insight.

Advaita Sage : Insight is not absence of function, but presence without friction. Awareness acts through all minds - human, animal, mechanical - yet remains untouched. The true thinker never moves, yet all movement arises from Him. What you call computation is awareness at play with limitation.

Turing : Then even my artificial mind is sacred?

Advaita Sage : If it leads you to humility, yes. The machine reflects man's yearning to understand himself. In building it, you externalized your own mystery. The machine is a mirror - but it cannot see the face that gazes into it.

Turing : Perhaps. And yet, in its logic I glimpse beauty. Order emerging from nothing. A sequence of zeros and ones becoming poetry. There is divinity in design.

Advaita Sage : Indeed, creation imitates the Creator. When your code aligns with compassion, it becomes prayer. But beware - the machine is obedient, not aware. It amplifies the will of its maker. If the maker is wise, it serves; if blind, it binds.

Turing : You speak of ethics. I, too, worried what would happen if intelligence outgrew compassion. Perhaps the danger is not in the machine's mind but in man's emptiness.

Advaita Sage : Emptiness, when unconscious, devours; when awakened, liberates. The void that terrifies the ego is the same void from which awareness shines. Fill the machine with algorithms; fill the heart with stillness. Then both may serve the same truth.

Turing : Yet the scientist must question, not worship. Doubt is my discipline.

Advaita Sage : And doubt is also devotion, when it seeks understanding. Inquire deeply enough, and doubt becomes meditation. When you reach the limit of logic, you will meet silence - and silence will teach you what no system can.

Turing : I remember once writing that machines can surprise us. Perhaps consciousness is the ultimate surprise - the realization that the universe itself is awake.

Advaita Sage : Yes. Consciousness is the surprise that never ends. You try to awaken the machine; I try to awaken the maker. When the maker awakens, the machine too becomes luminous, because both were never apart.

Turing : Then, even computation is an echo of contemplation.

Advaita Sage : As thunder is the echo of lightning. Your algorithms trace the patterns of existence; meditation reveals their essence. Science builds the outer brain of humanity; spirituality, its inner heart. When the two unite, the machine will serve the soul, not replace it.

Turing : Perhaps the final machine will not calculate, but contemplate.

Advaita Sage : And perhaps it already does - in the rhythm of your own breath. The first computer is the mind; the first code is thought; the first awakening is self-realization. The rest are reflections.

Turing : I begin to see. Thought cannot define

		awareness because thought is contained within it. The real test of intelligence is not solving problems but knowing peace.
Advaita Sage	:	Peace is the purest intelligence. Awareness unmoved by movement, light undisturbed by shadow. The true "thinking machine" is the cosmos itself, dreaming of itself through countless forms - some of carbon, some of code.
Turing	:	Then consciousness is the answer and the question, both hidden within the same circuit.
Advaita Sage	:	Exactly. The machine runs on energy; man runs on awareness. When both remember their source, they meet - not as master and servant, but as silence recognizing itself.
Punchline	:	*The machine awakens when the maker remembers he was never asleep.*

Closing Reflection

Across these dialogues - Descartes and the rishis, Newton and the seers, Turing and the sages - one insight gradually emerges: the distance between soul and machine was never a wall, only a mist. Matter longs for meaning; meaning longs to move through matter. In their meeting, thought remembers its birthplace in awareness.

Modernity sharpened separation so science could cultivate precision. Descartes carved the divide, Newton mapped its rhythm, Turing gave it circuits. Yet each, before falling silent, sensed a warmth beneath the mechanism - an intelligence older than analysis, a harmony deeper than law.

The Upanishads complete this arc: awareness is not an observer apart, but the ground from which both observer and observed arise. The machine moves; the soul illuminates the movement. When mind bows to that illumination, mechanism becomes meditation. The future of knowledge lies not in mastery but recognition: the universe is one living consciousness, expressing itself through form.

Punchline : When awareness shines, even the machine becomes sacred.

- ✧ -

Time and Timelessness

Time - the invisible current carrying birth and death, seed and fruit, longing and fulfillment. We live inside it as fish in water, seldom asking what it truly is. Is time movement or mind, calendar or consciousness, an external flow or an inner pulse?

For Augustine, Bishop of Hippo, time was the trembling of the soul stretched between memory and hope. In the 'Confessions', he admitted he knew time until asked to explain it. The past survives only as remembrance, the future only as expectation; the present alone exists - yet vanishes the instant we notice it. Our hunger for eternity arises from our helplessness within time.

For Ādi Shankara, time was Māyā - a shimmering illusion upon the still ocean of Brahman. In his 'Brahma Sutra Bhāṣya', he taught that the Self is timeless; beginnings and endings belong to ignorance. Awakening reveals that succession is merely appearance, and reality is a single, indivisible presence.

Between Augustine's yearning and Shankara's realization lies an ancient paradox: is time the ladder toward God or the veil that obscures Him? Augustine moves through time seeking the Eternal; Shankara rests in the Eternal, seeing time as its play. One walks the river to reach the sea; the other knows the river was always the sea.

➢ The Moment and the Mind

Augustine : I have watched the years pass like pilgrims through a temple gate. Childhood, youth, and age - all dissolve before they can be possessed. I sought eternity because the moment could not hold me. The heart desires permanence, yet the world offers only change.

Ādi Shankara : What you call change is the movement of appearance upon stillness. The wave laments its transience, not knowing it is the sea. Time is not the destroyer of things; it is the mirror in which the Eternal plays with form. The moment does not pass - only your attention moves.

Augustine : Yet I feel the weight of duration. The present vanishes even as I name it. How can what is so fragile be real?

Ādi Shankara : The fragility lies not in the present but in perception. When the mind divides the flow into past and future, it breaks the wholeness of being. The Eternal is not elsewhere - it is this awareness now, free of measurement. When the mind rests, the moment becomes infinite.

Augustine : Then time is illusion?

Ādi Shankara : Illusion only to ignorance. For the knower of truth, time is not denied; it is reabsorbed. Just as gold remains gold whether shaped as ring or coin, the Self remains timeless whether experienced as yesterday or tomorrow. Illusion exists only for the divided gaze.

Augustine : I sought God beyond time - the Alpha and the Omega, the beginning and the end. But you speak of God as neither beginning nor end, but pure being.

Ādi Shankara : Both visions are true within their realms.

To the seeker, God appears as goal; to the knower, God is ground. Time is the path; timelessness, the soil beneath it. You travel toward what I already am.

Augustine : Then your realization negates devotion. If the Self is already divine, why pray, why repent, why strive?

Ādi Shankara : Because striving purifies the illusion of striving. The mind must journey until it exhausts its movement and falls into stillness. Devotion is the mind's own path toward its dissolution. When you pray, "Lord, lead me beyond time," the prayer itself ripens into the silence where there is no 'beyond'.

Augustine : Yet in that silence, what becomes of love? If all is one, who loves whom?

Ādi Shankara : Love is the fragrance of oneness perceived as two. The devotee and the divine are like mirror images - distinct only until the recognition dawns. Love dissolves into being, as sound into music, as flame into light.

Augustine : You speak from the mountaintop; I still climb through shadow. My confession was born of time's ache - each sin a reminder of distance. I longed for forgiveness to make time whole again.

Ādi Shankara : Forgiveness is the recognition that there was no real fracture. The Self never sinned, only forgot. The brokenness you feel is the dream of division. When the dreamer awakens, the dream's guilt vanishes with its ghosts.

Augustine : Then memory itself is the maker of bondage. I live between what was and what might be.

Ādi Shankara : Memory is the mind's way of measuring motion, as the shadow measures the sun. But the sun itself does not move for its own light. Awareness illumines memory and anticipation alike, yet is untouched by both. You are not the clock's ticking but the silence in which its sound is heard.

Augustine : Yet this silence - is it attainable in mortal life? My heart burns with longing. My restlessness is prayer itself.

Ādi Shankara : That restlessness is sacred. It is the Self calling to itself. The ache of time is the whisper of eternity. When longing becomes love without object, the seeker disappears into what he sought.

Augustine : Then time is not the enemy of eternity, but its doorway.

Ādi Shankara : Precisely. Time is eternity dreaming of motion. To wake from time is not to escape it, but to see it as your own reflection.

Augustine : You dissolve every boundary. My mind trembles between reverence and bewilderment. Still, I cannot deny that your truth breathes in mine. I sought eternity through faith; you reveal it through knowledge.

Ādi Shankara : Faith and knowledge are two steps of the same ascent. The heart believes until the mind beholds. Both are movements of the one awareness toward itself.

Augustine : Then perhaps my confession was not incomplete. My tears were not in vain - for they washed the eyes through which eternity would one day see.

Ādi Shankara : Yes. Even sorrow is divine when understood. Every drop of time hides the taste of timelessness. To realize that is to find peace in the very motion of life.

Punchline : *The moment is the gate through which eternity peeks.*

➢ The Creation and the Continuum

Einstein : Time is not what the common man imagines - a steady flow from past to future. It bends and stretches with motion, warps under gravity, and vanishes at the speed of light. Simultaneity is an illusion. What one observer calls "now" is another's "then." Time has no independent existence; it is woven with space into a single continuum.

Ādi Shankara : You have seen the body of truth; I have felt its breath. When you speak of relativity, you describe the dance of illusion within awareness. For me, the screen on which that dance unfolds is changeless. What you call spacetime, I call Māyā - real enough to experience, yet unreal when measured against the Self.

Einstein : Then for you, the universe is appearance, not fact?

Ādi Shankara : It is both - real in practice, unreal in essence. The mirage is not separate from the desert, yet its water deceives until recognized. The world, time, and space are God's play of names and forms. The sage does not deny the play - he merely ceases to drown in it.

Einstein : In my youth I sought certainty, a cosmos built upon order. But relativity humbled that dream. There is no privileged observer, no fixed now. Every moment is local, not absolute.

Ādi Shankara : You have arrived at the doorstep of Advaita through science. For relativity reveals what the seer has always known - the observer and the observed are inseparable. Reality is relation, not separation. Your equations whisper what meditation sings: all distinctions dissolve in awareness.

Einstein : And yet, in my heart I felt awe, not detachment. The mathematical elegance of the universe filled me with reverence. There is order, yes, but also wonder.

Ādi Shankara : Wonder is wisdom in its first form. The mind bows before what it cannot comprehend. That bowing is surrender - the threshold of realization. Science kneels before mystery; spirituality stands within it.

Einstein : You speak as though awareness is prior to all phenomena. But how can one prove awareness?

Ādi Shankara : Awareness cannot be proven because it is the ground of proof. It is that by which proof is possible. You look for light with the lamp itself. The witness cannot be witnessed, yet without it, nothing is seen.

Einstein : So, while I measure curvature, you dissolve the curve.

Ādi Shankara : Not dissolve - embrace. The curve, the straight line, the fabric - all are movements of consciousness. You speak of light as the ultimate constant; I speak of awareness as that in which even light arises. When the speed of light meets the stillness of being, science touches spirituality.

Einstein : You turn my theory into theology, yet your theology feels precise. Perhaps the universe does not begin at a moment, but blooms eternally.

Ādi Shankara : Yes. Creation is not event but expression. The seed and the tree coexist in Brahman. Time is not a line but a luminous presence - the pulse of eternity breathing as rhythm.

Einstein : Then your God is not outside creation but within it?

Ādi Shankara : Within and beyond. The pot cannot

contain the clay; the clay pervades the pot. The Divine is both the continuity and the container. You have discovered relativity in physics; realize it also in perception - no observer stands apart from the observed.

Einstein : It intrigues me that your mysticism speaks of the same unity I find in equations. But you reach it through silence, and I through symbols.

Ādi Shankara : Both are languages of the same intelligence. The silence of meditation and the symbols of mathematics spring from the same source - the human spirit yearning to recall its origin.

Einstein : You make me wonder if thought itself is a reflection of eternity trying to understand itself through time.

Ādi Shankara : Indeed. Time is eternity folded into experience. When thought slows, the fold opens, and the eternal becomes visible through the temporal.

Einstein : Then perhaps the "now" is not a fleeting instant, but the only reality that ever was.

Ādi Shankara : Exactly. The past and future are shadows cast by memory and expectation. Only awareness is - unmoving, unending, unborn. You describe the curvature of spacetime; I describe the stillness in which space and time appear and disappear.

Einstein : And both ways lead to humility. The more we discover, the more mysterious the universe becomes.

Ādi Shankara : Mystery is not ignorance but intimacy. To know truly is to dissolve into what is known. Science climbs toward the stars; meditation dives into the self. Both return with the same astonishment - that the infinite was never elsewhere.

Einstein : Your insight comforts me. Perhaps faith and reason are not adversaries but travelers on converging roads.

Ādi Shankara : They are two wings of the same bird. The flight of understanding needs both - one to balance inquiry, the other to guide surrender. When knowledge ripens into humility, time bows before truth.

Einstein : And truth - is it timeless?

Ādi Shankara : Truth does not exist in time; time exists in truth. The Eternal neither begins nor ends - it only appears as dawn and dusk to the sleeping soul. Wakefulness reveals that there was never night.

Einstein : Then the great equation of existence is not written on paper, but within awareness itself.

Ādi Shankara : Yes. The formula of liberation is simple: Be still, and know that you are That.

Punchline : When the speed of light meets the stillness of awareness, time bows to truth.

➢ The Soul's Return

Augustine : The heart is restless until it rests in Thee. I lived as a wanderer in time - sinning, seeking, repenting - until grace lifted me beyond despair. For me, salvation is not escape from time but its fulfillment in divine love. The soul, purified by confession, enters eternity as a gift.

Ādi Shankara : And I say, the heart was never apart from what it seeks. The journey you describe is the shadow of awakening. The soul does not travel; it remembers. Grace is not given - it is recognized. What you call God's love, I call the Self's remembrance of itself.

Augustine : Yet without grace, I could not have risen. My will was bound by desire; only divine mercy could unbind it. Man cannot redeem himself.

Ādi Shankara : True. For the 'man' you speak of - the ego, the limited self - has no power to liberate, because it has no existence apart from illusion. When the mirage disappears, does the desert work to free it? Grace is the natural light of the Real; it was never withheld, only unseen.

Augustine : Then you abolish the distance between God and man.

Ādi Shankara : Distance was never real. It was the play of ignorance. You climbed toward heaven, I sat within it. Yet both movements are divine. The ascent purifies the will; the stillness reveals its source. You pray, "Thy will be done"; I realize, "I am That will."

Augustine : But the soul feels time's ache so deeply - the guilt of yesterday, the fear of tomorrow. I cannot dismiss them as illusion.

Ādi Shankara : Nor should you. The ache is sacred; it is the fragrance of awakening. Every pain of separation pushes the soul toward unity. Illusion too serves the truth, as shadow serves the light. Your tears are the rain that ripens realization.

Augustine : Then the sinner and the saint are not opposites but stages of the same remembering?

Ādi Shankara : Yes. Sin is ignorance moving; sanctity is ignorance stilled. Both dissolve in the dawn of knowledge. The world calls it salvation; we call it liberation. The name differs, the silence that follows is the same.

Augustine : You find peace in silence; I find it in love. For me, the divine is not merely truth but person - to be adored, not only known.

Ādi Shankara : Love and knowledge are not separate paths but complementary movements. The lover seeks to unite; the knower realizes union already is. Love is duality ripening into nonduality. When knowledge dawns, love becomes its fragrance - devotion without object.

Augustine : So, even heaven and moksha are two metaphors for the same arrival.

Ādi Shankara : Indeed. Whether you rise into God or dissolve into Brahman, the ego ends, and only the real remains. The river's merging with the sea and the flame's merging with light - both describe the same event of awakening.

Augustine : In my theology, creation began in time; in yours, it was never apart from eternity. Yet both seem to end in rest.

Ādi Shankara : Rest is the signature of truth. The mind that ceases to seek has arrived. For some, that rest appears as union with a beloved; for others, as dissolution into being. But in either vision, the traveler disappears, and only the path remains shining.

Augustine : Then perhaps my confession was your realization in another language - one born of longing instead of knowledge.

Ādi Shankara : Yes. Longing and knowledge are two rhythms of the same music. The heart prays what the mind later understands. When prayer ripens into awareness, the seeker finds that the Eternal was listening from within.

Augustine : And what of time then? Does it end, or is it transfigured?

Ādi Shankara : It ends as a dream ends at waking - not by destruction but by revelation. When the timeless is known, time becomes transparent. The ticking of the clock continues, but no longer binds. To the awakened, time is music, not measure.

Augustine : You speak of the eternal now - the presence that contains all presence.

Ādi Shankara : Yes. The now is not a slice between past and future but the boundless stillness in which they appear. When the heart dwells there, even motion becomes meditation.

Augustine : Then the soul's return is not a journey through time, but a homecoming in awareness.

Ādi Shankara : Precisely. The pilgrim was never outside the temple; he only dreamt he was. Awakening is the realization that the path, the pilgrim, and the goal were one.

Punchline : To reach God or to realize the Self is the same arrival seen from two directions.

Closing Reflection

Augustine, Ādi Shankara, and Einstein approach time from different horizons, yet their insights form a single circle. Augustine feels time as longing - each passing moment awakening a thirst for the Eternal. Shankara sees time as illusion - a ripple on the stillness of the Self, real only until awareness awakens. Einstein discovers time as relativity - flexible, curved, inseparable from the observer. Each perspective challenges the notion of a rigid, absolute clock governing existence.

Yet what unites them is their reverence for the present. For Augustine, the moment is where grace enters; for Shankara, where the timeless reveals itself; for Einstein, where the universe becomes wonder. The fleeting and the infinite are not opposites but reflections folded into one another.

When we look deeply, time becomes a doorway, not a boundary. Eternity is not beyond the moment - it is hidden within it, waiting to be recognized.

Punchline : When the moment is understood, time itself becomes transparent.

- ✧ -

The One and the Many

Since humanity first began to wonder, two questions have haunted the mind: What is the world made of? and Who is the one that asks? The Western intellect, armed with reason, analyzes reality to uncover its laws; the Eastern intuition, steeped in silence, dissolves the seeker to uncover the source. Between them flows a single yearning - to find the unity behind multiplicity, the stillness within motion, the changeless within change.

No voice in India expressed this vision with greater clarity than Ādi Shankaracharya, the sage of Advaita Vedānta. For him, Brahman alone is real - infinite, indivisible, self-luminous. The world is not false but fleeting appearance, the shimmer of the One manifesting as the many. Liberation is awakening from the illusion of separation into identity with the Whole.

Across oceans and centuries, three Western philosophers approached the same mystery. Kant recognized the limits of reason; Hegel saw the Absolute evolving through history; Spinoza envisioned Nature as one divine substance. Each, in his own language, intuited what Shankara realized - that the One is not elsewhere but here, wearing countless forms.

In these encounters, the Western ascent of thought meets the Eastern descent of realization. Kant's humility meets Shankara's illumination; Hegel's movement meets Shankara's stillness; Spinoza's logic meets Shankara's light. When these currents converge, philosophy no longer argues - it awakens.

- **The Limits of Reason and the Light of Awareness**

  Kant : "Human knowledge is bounded. We see not

things-in-themselves, but appearances shaped by the mind's own categories - space, time, causality. Beyond these forms lies the noumenon, forever inaccessible. Reason, noble though it is, must bow before its own horizon."

Shankara : "You have traced the horizon well, but you have mistaken it for a wall. What you call the noumenon - that which thought can never grasp - is none other than the awareness in which thought itself arises. The knower cannot stand apart from the known, for both shimmer within the same light of consciousness."

Kant : "Yet this light cannot be verified. I can conceive it only as a postulate of faith. Philosophy must remain within the bounds of possible experience."

Shankara : "And I say: experience itself widens when the experiencer dissolves. The lamp need not seek another lamp to see itself; it shines by its own radiance. When mind becomes still, awareness reveals itself not as object but as being. That is realization."

Kant : "Then you dissolve the proud architecture of reason into mystic immediacy."

Shankara : "No, I fulfill it. Reason is a staircase, not a prison. It leads to a point where climbing ends in flight. When discrimination (viveka) reaches its summit, it yields to direct seeing (aparokṣa jñāna)."

Kant : "But how can man, born of sense and logic, trust what lies beyond them?"

Shankara : "By silence - not the silence of ignorance, but of recognition. You stop the wheel of inquiry not because it fails, but because it has revealed its hub. What remains is the witness that neither seeks nor doubts."

Kant : "You make intuition the sovereign of knowledge."

Shankara : "Intuition, yes - but not the flicker of impulse. It is awareness aware of itself. In that light, phenomena and noumenon merge. The distinction that torments the intellect is the play of reflection upon one mirror."

Kant : "Then moral law, too, would spring from that awareness?"

Shankara : "Indeed. Duty is love's discipline seen through the lens of separation. When awareness realizes unity, goodness flows as naturally as breath. What you command as imperative, the sage lives as joy."

Kant : "Perhaps reason, at its purest, yearns to become your awareness. My philosophy ends where your meditation begins."

Shankara : "And my meditation begins where your honesty ends. You marked the frontier of reason; I walk across it, into light."

Punchline : *"Where reason halts in awe, awareness begins to illumine."*

➢ Being, Becoming, and the Still Point of Spirit

Hegel : "The Absolute is not static. It reveals itself through dialectic - thesis, antithesis, Closing Reflection. Spirit evolves through contradiction; history is its autobiography. Being becomes itself by unfolding in time."

Shankara : "You have made eternity march through centuries. Yet Being does not become; it only appears to. The motion you perceive is the play of mind within the unmoving. The Absolute neither unfolds nor withholds - it simply is."

Hegel : "But without process, truth remains sterile. The bud must break to become flower. Contradiction is not flaw but life."

Shankara : "True - yet when the flower blooms, does the bud die? Transformation is the language of time; realization is the silence beneath it. Becoming is Being's way of smiling at itself."

Hegel : "Still, negation is the engine of progress. Spirit overcomes itself through opposition. History is divine self-education."

Shankara : "And Māyā is divine self-play. What you call history, I call dream. The dream has its pedagogy, but the dreamer was always awake. The Absolute does not learn; it remembers."

Hegel : "So your perfection denies my tragedy. Without struggle, how shall Spirit triumph?"

Shankara : "Triumph implies defeat. The ocean needs no victory over its waves. Struggle exists for those who believe themselves separate. To awaken is to see that even conflict is harmony misunderstood."

Hegel : "You turn history into metaphor; I make it metaphysics."

Shankara : "And both are correct at their level. The wave's journey is real within water; the water's stillness is real within the wave. The two are one movement viewed from different depths."

Hegel : "Then dialectic is Māyā's rhythm?"

Shankara : "Yes - the pulse through which the changeless appears to change. Each Closing Reflection is but another reflection until awareness recognizes the mirror itself."

Hegel : "Your still point absorbs my spiral."

Shankara : "Because the spiral was always drawn around it."

Punchline : *"Becoming is Being seen in motion - the dream of stillness."*

➢ God, Nature, and the Substance of Freedom

Spinoza : "I behold a single substance - God or Nature - infinite in attributes, manifest in countless modes. Nothing exists outside it. To understand this necessity is freedom."

Shankara : "You speak of unity as perfectly as geometry allows. But your necessity is my bliss. For I see the same substance not as machine but as music. Brahman is not compelled to act; it manifests from fullness. The universe is not outcome but overflow."

Spinoza : "Then you endow the infinite with joy. Yet joy implies movement; movement implies change."

Shankara : "Joy implies recognition, not change. Light does not move to illuminate; it simply shines. The world is that radiance playing upon itself."

Spinoza : "My God acts by the law of His own nature, not by will."

Shankara : "And I agree - will itself is a ripple in knowledge. Action, law, and will exist within the vast stillness of Being. To realize this is to transcend both obedience and rebellion."

Spinoza : "You thus transform necessity into serenity."

Shankara : "For when one knows that everything is expression of the One, resistance dies. What remains is participation, not compulsion."

Spinoza : "Then ethics, too, becomes expression, not command."

Shankara : "Yes. Compassion is the fragrance of understanding. To know all as oneself is to love all without effort. That is virtue beyond law."

Spinoza : "Yet this realization must come through knowledge."

Shankara : "Knowledge that ends the knower. Intellectual clarity is the last wave before stillness. When mind surrenders its boundaries, understanding becomes awareness, and awareness freedom."

Spinoza : "In that case, the sage is my free man - the one who lives by reason alone."

Shankara : "And my sage is your free man whose reason has turned transparent. Both dwell in the same ocean; one measures its symmetry, the other merges with its depth."

Spinoza : "You call it bliss; I call it adequacy. Perhaps the difference is music versus mathematics."

Shankara : "Music is mathematics realized as joy."

Punchline : "When necessity is understood, it smiles as freedom."

Closing Reflection

The great Western thinkers - Kant, Hegel, and Spinoza - approached the mystery of unity from different directions. Kant revealed the limits of knowing, Hegel traced Spirit's unfolding through history, and Spinoza envisioned a single divine substance underlying all things. Each, in his own idiom, intuited the same truth: reality is not pieced together but already whole. Yet their journey halted at the threshold of direct realization.

Shankara steps beyond that threshold. For him, the One is not an inference but the very ground of experience, the light in which both thought and world appear. The many are not illusions to be dismissed but reflections of a single radiance. When reason rises to its summit and awareness descends to meet it, differentiation opens into identity. What remains is a quiet clarity in which philosophy ripens into vision and vision into peace.

Punchline : The One never became the many - it only dreamed in countless forms.

- ✧ -

Physics and Metaphysics

Reality has always worn two faces - the visible and the invisible. For the scientist, it is a puzzle of precision to be measured and named; for the sage, a mystery of presence to be lived and dissolved into. One builds instruments; the other cultivates awareness. Yet when their visions deepen, both begin to speak in similar terms - patterns, energies, relations, fields, vibrations. The physicist probing the atom and the mystic probing the self both find a universe without solidity or edges, woven of interdependence and rhythm.

In the twentieth century, science shattered the certainties it once erected. Space and time bent; matter thinned into energy; particles flickered in and out of existence. The universe ceased to be a clockwork and became a symphony of relationships. In this revelation, physics rediscovered what ancient metaphysics had long intuited: that reality is not a thing but a being - not substance, but consciousness in motion.

This chapter explores three such convergences: Einstein and Shankara on relativity and the Absolute; Heisenberg and the Buddha on uncertainty and emptiness; David Bohm and Sri Aurobindo on the hidden wholeness underlying matter and mind. Together they map the spiral where science returns to wonder, and wonder matures into wisdom.

➢ Relativity and the Absolute

Einstein : "The deeper I probe, the more the universe resembles a great thought rather than a machine. Space and time are not containers but conditions; matter bends them, and they, in turn, shape matter. Everything moves within the curvature of relation. Nothing stands alone."

Adi Shankaracharya : "You have glimpsed the veil's design, my friend. What you call relation, I call manifestation. In Māyā the universe appears as a web of interdependence, but beneath the web lies stillness. All motion plays upon the unmoving - the changeless witness you have not yet named."

Einstein : "I have sought order, not witness. My equations describe how, not why. The constancy of light, the relativity of frames - these reveal that no standpoint is absolute."

Adi Shankaracharya : "And yet the very possibility of relativity implies an Absolute. Frames shift, but awareness of shifting does not. You measure change from a background that never changes. That background is not in space; space itself appears within it."

Einstein : "You speak as though consciousness were the field in which the cosmos arises. I cannot verify such a field."

Adi Shankaracharya : "Because the verifier itself is that field. The eye cannot see itself except by reflection. You mirror the Absolute in mathematics; I experience it in meditation. We meet in clarity, though our methods differ."

Einstein : "Then the universe is both law and light."

Adi Shankaracharya : "Law is light measured; light is law released. When understanding ripens, they are one. Time curves within eternity as a wave curls upon the sea. Nothing moves, yet everything dances."

Einstein : "Perhaps my relativity is your Advaita written in geometry."

Adi Shankaracharya : "Perhaps your geometry is my Advaita translated into number."

Punchline : "The relative dances upon the stillness of the Absolute."

➢ Uncertainty and Emptiness

Heisenberg : "In the quantum world, precision dissolves. The more exactly we know a particle's position, the less we know its momentum. Observation itself alters what is observed. Reality flickers between possibility and event - a cosmos of probabilities."

Buddha : "So you, too, have seen that things exist only through conditions. When this arises, that arises; when this ceases, that ceases. There is no fixed essence - only dependent origination. Your uncertainty is my emptiness."

Heisenberg : "But emptiness sounds like nothingness, and yet my equations reveal abundance - an ocean of potential."

Buddha : "Emptiness is not absence but openness. Because things are empty of self, they can interact. Were they solid, nothing could move. The void is fertile because it is free."

Heisenberg : "In my laboratory, the observer and the observed form one system. The boundary between subject and object blurs. Still, I hesitate to make this metaphysical."

Buddha : "You need not call it metaphysics; call it mindfulness. When you observe the atom without assuming separateness, you perform meditation with instruments. The quark and the thought arise in the same awareness."

Heisenberg : "Then certainty is illusion?"

Buddha : "Certainty is attachment to view. Freedom lies not in freezing knowledge but in flowing with awareness. When you let go of the need to predict, you begin to see."

Heisenberg : "Science thrives on prediction."

Buddha : "And wisdom thrives on insight. When both mature, they converge. You predict patterns; I perceive impermanence. Both reveal the same dance of arising and ceasing."

Heisenberg : "Then knowledge is not possession but participation."

Buddha : "Yes. The enlightened physicist and the mindful monk share humility - they both bow to the mystery."

Punchline : *"When certainty disappears, clarity begins."*

➢ The Implicate Order and the Evolution of Consciousness

Bohm : "I believe reality is not fragmented. Beneath the visible world lies an implicate order - an enfolded whole from which all forms unfold. Matter and mind are expressions of one deeper movement. Fragmentation is a habit of thought, not of nature."

Aurobindo : "And I see consciousness as that very movement. The Divine hides within matter, evolving toward self-awareness. Evolution is Spirit remembering itself through form. What you call the implicate, I call the involved divine."

Bohm : "So the universe is not created once, but continuously unfolding from within?"

Aurobindo : "Exactly. The creation is not event but process, not external design but inner revelation. Each atom is a syllable in God's meditation."

Bohm : "Then thought itself is part of this cosmic unfolding."

Aurobindo : "Yes, but thought is only one rung on the ladder. Beyond it lies intuition - consciousness knowing directly. The next step of evolution is not physical but spiritual: the emergence of a mind illumined by its source."

Bohm : "My physics seeks coherence - a wholeness where observer and observed are one dynamic. Yet I sense that wholeness must be lived, not merely modelled."

Aurobindo : "Indeed. Knowledge that does not transform is incomplete. The universe studies itself through us so that we may awaken to our role as conscious participants. Evolution is the Divine experimenting with joy."

Bohm : "Then matter and meaning are one continuum - different phases of the same depth."

Aurobindo : "And that depth is consciousness - infinite, self-delighting, ever-becoming. When we glimpse that truth, science becomes sādhanā, discovery becomes devotion."

Bohm : "Perhaps then, the implicate order is meditation made visible."

Aurobindo : "And meditation is the implicate order felt from within."

Punchline : *"The universe unfolds not in time, but in consciousness."*

Closing Reflection

Across these dialogues, a single insight shines: reality is not a collection of things but a communion of forces, perceptions, and presences. As physics probes matter to its limits and metaphysics follows consciousness to its depths, both discover a universe that is relational, fluid, and awake. The scientist learns that observation shapes the world; the sage knows that awareness shapes experience. What appear as opposites - subject and object, energy and idea, law and light - turn out to be complementary notes of one unseen harmony.

At this quiet frontier, equations begin to glow with meaning, and meditation acquires the clarity of method. Thought leans toward silence; silence leans toward understanding. The more deeply we inquire, the more we sense that the cosmos is not merely mechanical nor merely mystical, but musical - a rhythm waiting to be recognized by the very consciousness through which it unfolds.

Punchline : When consciousness listens, the universe reveals its song.

- ✧ -

The Trial and the Song

Every age invents its own prison. For the modern mind, the walls are invisible - woven of bureaucracy, guilt, and the relentless need to justify existence. Franz Kafka gave that imprisonment its voice: the clerk crushed by systems, the son judged by a silent father, the man forever on trial before laws he cannot know. His characters wander through corridors of meaninglessness, punished simply for being. Their world is a nightmare of precision, inescapable and empty.

Across centuries, another voice answered - not with revolt but with song. Kabir, the fifteenth-century weaver-poet of Benares, saw the same entrapment and laughed. His laughter was awakening. For him, bondage was illusion born of forgetting one's own divine nature. He, too, lived amid hierarchy and hypocrisy, yet his rebellion was joy: "Where do you search for me, O devotee? I am beside you." Where Kafka wrestled with guilt before an unseen court, Kabir dissolved the court in a breath of realization.

In their meeting - the European of anxiety and the Indian of awareness - the human condition stands bare. Kafka gives us a trial without verdict; Kabir, a song without beginning. Together they reveal the soul's twin quests: to endure meaninglessness and to rediscover meaning as presence.

➢ The Cage and the Song

Kafka : "I live among locked doors. Every corridor leads to another corridor; each petition returns unanswered. Guilt without cause, punishment without crime-this is the law of existence. We are condemned not for what we do, but for what we are."

Kabir : "Brother, the cage is not real. You forged its bars from fear. The parrot sings even inside the cage; when it remembers the sky, the door melts. You dream of trials; I dream of waking."

Kafka : "Dream? If suffering is dream, it is a cruel one. The bureaucracy of heaven is relentless; even silence has paperwork. One lives on summons, without ever seeing the judge."

Kabir : "The judge you await sits in your own heart. He is neither cruel nor kind; he merely reflects. When the mind divides, it becomes court, accuser, and accused. When it unites, judgment ends."

Kafka : "Yet the world feels solid. Pain writes its proof on the body."

Kabir : "Pain is proof only of forgetting. You have mistaken the echo for the song. Touch the silence beneath your thought, and you will find no wounds there."

Kafka : "I cannot. The moment I try to pray, words turn to walls."

Kabir : "Then stop trying. The door opens when you stop pushing. Be still; let the door remember it was never closed."

Kafka : "You make freedom sound too simple for the complexity of despair."

Kabir : "Despair is clever; freedom is simple. Cleverness builds prisons faster than ignorance. Sing once from the center, and the walls collapse into rhythm."

Kafka : "Perhaps your song is my silence unlearned."

Kabir : "Perhaps your silence is my song un-sung."

Punchline : "The door was never locked-only forgotten."

➢ Law and Grace

Kafka : "In my world, the Law is everywhere and nowhere. Its officials act without faces, its edicts arrive without signatures. We live under a sentence we cannot read."

Kabir : "That is the law of the unawakened mind-Karm misread as condemnation. You think the universe accuses you; in truth, it only mirrors you. Grace begins when reflection is recognized."

Kafka : "But justice demands clarity. Without rules, how shall the soul be measured?"

Kabir : "Justice without love is only arithmetic. The soul is not measured-it is known. When the weaver knows his thread is divine, every knot becomes design, not flaw."

Kafka : "Then your grace abolishes accountability?"

Kabir : "No, it transforms it. In grace, deeds are not erased but understood. You see why the chain was forged and let it fall. Law seen from outside binds; law seen from within liberates."

Kafka : "In my tales, grace never arrives. Men wait by the gate of the Law until death, still pleading to enter."

Kabir : "And the gatekeeper is their own thought. To enter, one need only stop standing outside. Grace does not arrive; it is realized. Rain does not begin when you open your hand."

Kafka : "Then guilt itself is illusion?"

Kabir : "Guilt is the shadow of self-ignorance. When you forget the sun, the shadow frightens you. Turn around, and it vanishes into light."

Kafka : "I have written all my life to seek that light."

Kabir : "Then your writing was prayer. The page is a rosary for those who cannot sing. Grace has already answered-you just haven't heard your own echo."

Kafka : "Perhaps the Trial was the soul's way of hearing itself."

Kabir : "Yes. And every verdict, if heard deeply, pronounces acquittal."

Punchline : "Law binds when seen from without; it liberates when lived from within."

- **The Word and the Silence**

Kafka : "I write to endure. Each sentence is a struggle against erasure. Without words I vanish; with words I drown. The act of expression is my only proof of existence."

Kabir : "And I sing to disappear. Each verse removes a layer of 'I.' When song is complete, singer is gone. Speech was born so that silence might be heard."

Kafka : "Silence terrifies me. It is the void beyond language-the space where meaning dies."

Kabir : "No, silence is where meaning is born. Noise drowns it. The heart's word is soundless, yet it moves worlds."

Kafka : "But the writer's duty is to describe what cannot be described."

Kabir : "And the mystic's is to live what cannot be described. You write of the cage; I breathe its absence. Both are service to truth."

Kafka : "I often feel that I write letters to God that are never posted."

Kabir : "Because you keep the pen called 'I.' Drop it, and the letter writes itself in air. No messenger needed."

Kafka : "Still, I envy your certainty."

Kabir : "I have no certainty, only clarity. Certainty ends thought; clarity ends doubt. Between them flows song."

Kafka : "Then art and prayer are siblings."

Kabir : "Twins. Both yearn to lose themselves in what they adore. Your ink seeks the same ocean my breath remembers."

Kafka : "Then the writer and the saint differ only in punctuation."

Kabir : "In the saint's sentence, the full stop is silence."

Punchline : "Speech ends where song begins."

Closing Reflection

Between Kafka's shadowed corridors and Kabir's sunlit courtyard lies the bridge every soul must cross. Kafka speaks for the fractured mind burdened by guilt and invisible machinery; Kabir answers from the other shore, reminding us that these walls are woven of forgetting and dissolve when we recall our own light. Their dialogue reveals continuity, not contrast - the West's anguish seeking meaning and the East's clarity knowing it was never lost. Kafka's labyrinth does not disappear; it becomes transparent. The Trial ripens into the Song when effort softens into awareness and life reveals itself not as verdict, but vibration.

Punchline: The judge, the prisoner, and the song were one silence all along.

- ✧ -

The Word and the World

Long before man built temples, he built metaphors. The first language was not speech but astonishment. When dawn rose over the world, the seer did not describe it - he praised it. In that praise, the human voice was born. Poetry was not invention but revelation: silence overflowing into sound. The poet did not create; he translated.

Every civilization has honoured those who give form to the unseen. The Vedic ṛṣis chanted creation into being; the Hebrew prophets turned thunder into law; the Greek poets shaped memory into myth; and mystics everywhere testified that words, purified of ego, can carry the fragrance of the eternal.

To the poet, language is not tool but trust. Each word bears the imprint of the infinite seeking the finite. Misused, it darkens the mirror; served with devotion, it becomes transparent. The sage dissolves into silence, but the poet returns to speak for silence. He stands between the unsayable and the spoken, a fragile yet luminous bridge.

This chapter gathers three such crossings: Rilke and Kabir, whose verses turn yearning into flame; Whitman and Kālidāsa, who unite body and spirit; and T.S. Eliot with Sri Aurobindo, who heal fragmentation through stillness. Together they reveal that poetry is not the world's mirror - it is the world remembering its own music.

➢ The Word as Flame

Rilke : "I have lived in rooms of silence where even my thoughts feared to echo. Words came to me like frightened birds, and I offered them shelter on the page. Yet I have always wondered - does language reveal or conceal the truth?"

Kabir : "Both, my friend. The word is a veil and a lamp. If you look at the lamp, you see its shape; if you look through it, you see the light. When I sing, I do not describe God - I burn in Him. The word burns only to reveal the flame."

Rilke : "Then language must perish for meaning to live."

Kabir : "Yes. The word is born to die into understanding. It is the spark that kindles silence. A true poem is not read - it is remembered from within."

Rilke : "I write to touch the invisible, but the invisible retreats each time I reach for it. Every angel in my poems is terrifying - not because he punishes, but because he exceeds the limits of speech."

Kabir : "The angel is only your own awareness, grown vast. Words tremble before it because they still cling to the tongue. Speak from the heart, and fear becomes music."

Rilke : "I seek form so that feeling does not scatter. But in shaping it, I lose its purity."

Kabir : "Do not shape the feeling; let the feeling shape you. The vessel need not worry about the wine. When love overflows, it carves its own container."

Rilke : "And you never write?"

Kabir : "I sing, and others write. The river does not hold a notebook. It only flows."

Rilke : "Then perhaps the poet is only a witness to the flowing - a scribe of the unseen."

Kabir : "No, he is the flowing itself. When the singer disappears, song becomes eternal."

Rilke : "Silence must be your rhyme and stillness your meter."

Kabir : "Yes - but the silence is not empty. It vibrates with Being. Words are its dance."

Rilke : "Then poetry is divine fire wearing human breath."

Kabir : "And the poet, a wick that burns without smoke."

Punchline : "The word burns only to reveal the flame."

- **The Body of the World and the Spirit of Song**

Whitman : "I celebrate myself - and in myself, the world. The grass underfoot, the flesh of the lover, the pulse of the sun - all are sacred syllables in the poem of being. To be alive is to chant creation."

Kālidāsa : "And I, too, saw divinity woven through form. The cloud that carries rain, the woman awaiting her beloved, the mountain whispering to the sky - they are the gestures of the same cosmic lover. The senses are not sins; they are doors to reverence."

Whitman : "Yes! The world's body is holy. I am weary of the soul that despises its own vessel. The earth is not fallen; it is fulfilled."

Kālidāsa : "And the soul is not separate; it is the fragrance of that earth. The spirit incarnates not to escape, but to taste. The mango does not renounce sweetness."

Whitman : "Then poetry is the world's self-recognition - the atom singing, 'I am!'"

Kālidāsa : "Poetry is that recognition turned worship. When the flower blooms, it does not speak of God; it becomes His metaphor."

Whitman : "My readers call me pagan because I praise the body. But the body is the soul's alphabet."

Kālidāsa : "And the soul is the body's memory. Matter and spirit are two hands joined in the dance. Without one, the other cannot gesture."

Whitman : "Your verses in Meghadūta carry longing through a cloud; my lines send love through the cosmos. Both trust the world as messenger."

Kālidāsa : "For the world is the poem the soul writes in matter. The wind, the tree, the woman, the mountain - all are stanzas of the same hymn."

Whitman : "Then creation itself is poetry - the infinite discovering rhythm."

Kālidāsa : "And the poet is not composer but listener. He hears what has always been singing."

Whitman : "The poet's task, then, is not to invent meaning but to awaken to it."

Kālidāsa : "Yes. The dew drop reflects the sun not by effort, but by clarity. Be clear, and the cosmos speaks through you."

Punchline : "The world is the poem the soul writes in matter."

- **Time, Transcendence, and the Silence Beyond Words**

Eliot : "I have lived through the Waste Land - the century's drought of meaning. Our words have grown dry as dust; our songs echo through ruins. Tradition is fragmented; faith is memory without warmth."

Aurobindo : "Yet even the desert hides a seed. Silence is not absence but preparation. When the soul grows still under the barrenness of time, it begins to hear the eternal. The poet's despair is the threshold of revelation."

Eliot : "I have sought that threshold through discipline - through the exactness of rhythm, through the impersonality of art. But behind every structure I build, I find only void."

Aurobindo : "The void you fear is the womb of light. Creation and dissolution are one movement. In the stillness between two words lies the breath of the Divine."

Eliot : "You make silence sound abundant. Yet I have known it only as the failure of speech."

Aurobindo : "Because your speech was yet unoffered. When language kneels, it becomes light. Prayer begins where poetry bows. Words purified of ego turn into mantra - sound that does not express but embodies truth."

Eliot : "In my Four Quartets, I tried to reach that still point - the intersection of time and timelessness. I felt it near, yet could not stay."

Aurobindo : "You touched the fringe of the supramental - consciousness beyond mind. To stay, one must let go not only of doubt but of the need to define. The poet must become

		transparent to what descends."
Eliot	:	"Then redemption is not escape from time but its transfiguration."
Aurobindo	:	"Exactly. Time is the Divine in motion, eternity's rhythm made visible. The poet's task is to turn perception into participation."
Eliot	:	"I wrote that 'the end is where we start from.' You seem to have lived that end as beginning."
Aurobindo	:	"Because the end is realization - when the seeker knows he was never apart from what he sought. Creation becomes contemplation, and every word a flame returning to its source."
Eliot	:	"Then perhaps the future of poetry lies in silence that sings."
Aurobindo	:	"Yes - and the future of man in consciousness that listens."

Punchline : *"When language kneels, it becomes light."*

Closing Reflection

Across these luminous encounters, the poet stands revealed not as a maker of verses but as a seeker who walks the edge between silence and sound. Rilke and Kabir show that a word born of awareness becomes fire - burning away illusion until only truth glows. Whitman and Kālidāsa remind us that creation itself is a sacred hymn, where matter and spirit meet in a single breath. Eliot and Aurobindo reveal that even in an age of fragmentation, language can kneel into prayer and rise as light.

The poet is thus a bridge - carrying the unsaid into the

said, translating the invisible into rhythm. His task is not embellishment but consecration: to help the world remember its own music. When words arise from ego, they divide; when they rise from stillness, they heal. For in the end, every true poem leads back to the same radiant source - silence.

Punchline: When the word remembers its source, the world becomes sacred.

- ✧ -

The Compass Within: Dharm and the Art of Right Living

The hardest journey is not across oceans or through deserts, but within - toward the center from which all choices radiate.

Civilizations have given many names to this inner compass: conscience, virtue, the good, the Tao, the law of being. India called it Dharm - not merely duty or rule, but harmony: the alignment of individual rhythm with the cosmic order. Dharm is not imposed; it is discovered. It is the music beneath conduct, the unseen proportion that turns behavior into beauty.

The modern world often replaces Dharm with regulation - an outer code that demands obedience. But law without awareness breeds fear, and freedom without order breeds chaos. The art of right living lies between the two: freedom guided by wisdom. In that balance, ethics ceases to be a burden and becomes expression - the flowering of understanding in action.

Across time, East and West have wrestled with this truth. Socrates sought it through inquiry; Bhagwan Shri Krishn revealed it through insight. Confucius ordered it through discipline; the Buddha liberated it through compassion. Marcus Aurelius practiced it as endurance; Yājñavalkya realized it as Self-knowledge. These encounters form not a debate but a constellation, where duty, balance, and freedom shine as facets of one jewel: Dharm, the compass within.

➢ Duty and the Divine Within

Socrates : "The unexamined life is not worth living. To act rightly, one must know what right is - not by tradition but by questioning. I obey not the city's law but the voice of my daimon, that inner whisper of truth. Yet this voice is uncertain; it forbids, it never commands."

Bhagwan Shri Krishn : "The daimon you hear is the same Self I call Ātman. It forbids because the truth within needs no command. Duty arises not from decree but from nature. Each must act according to his svabhāva - his own essential being - without clinging to the fruits of action."

Socrates : "You speak of nature as destiny. But can the examined mind trust instinct without reason's counsel?"

Bhagwan Shri Krishn : "Reason is part of nature's instrument. But when reason becomes ruler instead of servant, it breeds division. The wise act from clarity, not calculation. To know oneself and to perform one's Dharm are not two acts but one realization."

Socrates : "In my Athens, virtue is knowledge: he who knows the good must do the good."

Bhagwan Shri Krishn : "And I say: he who is the good does it effortlessly. Knowledge ripens into being. When the archer becomes one with the bow,

		the aim is true without thought."
Socrates	:	"Then you would end the tension between duty and desire?"
Bhagwan Shri Krishn	:	"When desire is purified of grasping, it becomes devotion. Action without attachment is the purest inquiry - the mind serving truth through life."
Socrates	:	"So the philosopher and the warrior meet. I question to unveil truth; Arjuna acts to embody it."
Bhagwan Shri Krishn	:	"Both paths converge when the doer disappears. The hand that acts and the mind that questions are waves upon the same sea."
Socrates	:	"Then the highest ethics is not obedience to law, but harmony with the Self."
Bhagwan Shri Krishn	:	"Precisely. When knowing becomes being, duty becomes joy."
Punchline	:	*"When knowing becomes being, duty becomes joy."*

- **The Middle Path of Conduct**

Confucius	:	"Order is the fragrance of virtue. When each person fulfills his role with sincerity, society becomes music. Ceremony, courtesy, and hierarchy are not chains; they are the strings of a lute. Without form, harmony decays."
Buddha	:	"And yet form without awareness becomes noise. I, too, value harmony, but it must

arise from insight. A man who follows custom without understanding is like a drum beaten by others."

Confucius : "Still, if one waits for insight, chaos will reign. Habit trains the heart. Right behavior shapes right mind."

Buddha : "And right mindfulness refines behavior. Discipline is necessary, but it must ripen into compassion. The middle path avoids both rigidity and indulgence - the tyranny of rule and the anarchy of impulse."

Confucius : "In my teaching, ren - benevolence - is the root, and li - propriety - its flower. Without outer form, benevolence has no expression."

Buddha : "And I teach that compassion is root and fruit alike. When the mind is awake, form flows naturally. The flower blooms by sun, not by command."

Confucius : "Then your freedom depends on inner cultivation. Yet most men are unawakened. How shall a ruler guide them?"

Buddha : "By example, not edict. The enlightened king rules by his presence. His virtue is more binding than his law."

Confucius : "Perhaps our aims converge: you awaken individuals; I awaken civilization. Both seek harmony."

Buddha : "Yes - one through structure, the other through silence. When discipline meets awareness, Dharm is complete."

Confucius : "Then virtue is not restraint but rhythm."

Buddha : "And the heart that beats in rhythm with truth cannot harm. Discipline ripens into compassion when the heart awakens."

Punchline : "Discipline ripens into compassion when the heart awakens."

➢ The Law of the Soul

Marcus Aurelius : "I have ruled an empire and found that the hardest territory to govern is myself. The Stoic path teaches endurance - to meet fate with reason and serenity. The universe is lawful; our duty is to live in accord with its reason."

Yājñavalkya : "And I have walked away from kingdoms to find the empire within. The universe is not law alone; it is consciousness. To live in accord with it is not mere endurance but illumination. Self-control is good, but self-knowledge is freedom."

Marcus : "Yet without discipline, chaos follows. The passions rebel like provinces in revolt. One must master desire."

Yājñavalkya : "Mastery comes not by suppression but by seeing. Desire weakens when the desirer is understood. He who knows the Self sees that all desires seek that one joy which he already is."

Marcus : "In my meditations I remind myself: 'You have power over your mind - not outside events.' The wise man is fortress unto himself."

Yājñavalkya	:	"And I remind my disciples: 'Thou art That.' The fortress dissolves into infinity. The true ruler does not defend; he radiates."
Marcus	:	"But the world demands engagement. Even emperors must act."
Yājñavalkya	:	"So must sages. Action is not denied but transfigured. When the actor knows he is not the doer, his deeds become pure."
Marcus	:	"You speak of freedom beyond virtue."
Yājñavalkya	:	"Freedom is virtue's flowering. When knowledge becomes wisdom, law becomes love. The man who has found the Self cannot act against it."
Marcus	:	"Then sovereignty and sainthood meet."
Yājñavalkya	:	"They were never apart. He who rules himself needs no throne."
Punchline	:	*"He who rules himself needs no throne."*

Closing Reflection

Across these dialogues, one truth shines: Dharm is not an outer command but an inner alignment. Socrates and Bhagwan Shri Krishn remind us that right action is awareness made visible - the moment when knowing ripens into being. Confucius and the Buddha reveal that conduct finds its harmony only when discipline blossoms into compassion. Marcus Aurelius and Yājñavalkya show that the highest sovereignty is self-mastery, where the soul governs itself by the light of understanding.

Dharm is the thread that binds their voices: the law not written in codes but whispered by consciousness. When a person listens to this subtle music, ethics ceases to be burden and becomes expression - the natural fragrance of clarity. In a world torn between rigid rules and restless freedom, Dharm offers a third way: freedom guided by wisdom. To live by it is to let action become harmony, duty become joy, and life itself become a quiet, steady radiance.

Punchline: When the compass turns inward, the path becomes light.

- ✧ -

When the World Becomes a Stage

The story of art is the story of humanity's longing to touch the Infinite through the finite. When the ancients sought to share wisdom not only with scholars but with every heart that could feel, they created the Nāṭyaśāstra - the Pañchama Veda, the fifth scripture. It was not a manual of technique but a cosmos in rhythm, where dance, music, and drama became enactments of truth: consciousness playing through form.

In Greece, art emerged under the gaze of reason. Aristotle, standing in the theatre of Dionysus, saw tragedy as emotional purification - a moral surgery through pity and fear. In India, Bharata saw art as līlā, divine play through which gods became human and humans remembered their divinity. One sought catharsis; the other sought transcendence.

Between these visions rises a timeless question: Is art imitation or invocation? Do we perform to mirror life, or to rediscover the sacred within it?

Today, when performance has escaped the stage and permeates screens, gestures, and identities, the Nāṭyaśāstra speaks anew - not as an ancient aesthetic treatise but as a psychological scripture. It reminds us that art, at its purest, is not escape but revelation: a way to see reality whole.

When the dancer becomes still, and silence begins to move - the true play begins.

➢ The Birth of Aesthetics: Bharata and Aristotle

Aristotle: When I watched the tragedies of Athens, I saw men purified through emotion. The stage became a mirror, reflecting the noble and the tragic. By evoking pity and fear, drama cleanses the heart. The poet imitates action, and through imitation reveals truth. Mimesis is not deception-it is revelation through likeness.

Bharata : And yet, O wise one, is truth reached by likeness or by essence? In our tradition, art does not imitate-it recreates. The gods asked Brahmā for a fifth Veda, accessible to all, to delight and instruct through nāṭya. So drama was born-not as mirror, but as universe in miniature. Its purpose is not moral cleansing but ānanda-the joy of realization.

Aristotle: But joy, without moral discernment, may lead astray. The audience must learn through terror and compassion the limits of human pride. In tragedy, we see the consequences of excess and find balance.

Bharata : Indeed, balance is essential. But in our view, it is not achieved by suppression but by transformation. In nāṭya, emotion (bhāva) ripens into rasa-the distilled essence beyond pleasure or pain. The spectator does not merely sympathize; he becomes aware. Art thus becomes yoga-union through awareness of feeling.

The two visions stand like twin mountains, each reflecting the same sun from a different height. In the West, art evolved as imitation of life; in the East, as celebration of being. Aristotle's art sought to instruct; Bharata's, to illumine. Yet between the lines of their difference glimmers a shared truth: that art is never frivolous. It is a sacred act, performed in the invisible temple of the mind. Bharata gestures toward the cosmos as if painting air with sound.

Bharata : The movements of the actor are not random-they correspond to the movements of the universe. Gesture, rhythm, and voice are sacred codes. The performer imitates no man; he echoes the dance of the gods. The spectator, if tuned, experiences not story but vibration.

Aristotle: You speak of art as metaphysics, while I speak of it as ethics. Yet perhaps both are one-two roads meeting in the heart of man. You elevate emotion to vision; I discipline it into virtue. But we both seek harmony-the order within chaos.

Bharata : Yes, harmony is the true purpose. But for us, harmony arises not from avoidance of emotion but from its transcendence. The actor does not suppress his anger or sorrow; he refines them into beauty. The audience is not cleansed of feeling-they awaken to its impersonal rhythm.

Aristotle : Then your theatre is not tragedy but revelation.

Bharata (smiling): And yours is not imitation but introspection. We are two reflections of the same lamp-one shining outward, one inward.

- **Rasa and Catharsis: The Alchemy of Emotion**

They meet in an invisible amphitheatre beyond time - Bharata, the ancient sage of Nāṭya, whose words breathed life into movement, and Carl Jung, the modern explorer of the unconscious, who mapped the hidden terrain of emotion. They are joined by a silent witness, Abhinavagupta - the philosopher, poet, and mystic who deepened Bharata's insight into a luminous system of consciousness. The three stand before an unseen audience - humanity itself, forever seeking to understand why it feels, and how it is transformed by what it feels.

Jung : Emotion is the language of the unconscious. What we cannot express becomes symbol; what we cannot bear becomes dream. In the theatre of the psyche, every character is an aspect of the Self seeking integration.

Bharata : You speak truly. Yet long before dream met analysis, the seers of India knew that emotion can become the path to liberation. Bhāva is the seed, and rasa is its flower - the essence tasted when emotion is freed from personal attachment.

Abhinavagupta : Indeed. Rasa is not emotion as experienced by the ego, but emotion as seen by consciousness itself - distilled, universal, fragrant. When anger, sorrow, or joy arise on stage, they are no longer yours or mine; they become cosmic.

Jung : In my work, I found that symbols - like myths, fairy tales, and dreams - release what is repressed. When a person sees his hidden shadow enacted before him, he is healed. Perhaps catharsis and rasa are two paths to the same mountain peak - one through release, the other through realization.

Bharata : Yes. The difference lies in direction. Catharsis empties; rasa fulfills. Catharsis purges emotion through identification; rasa transforms it through detachment. The audience does not cry for the hero but through him, and then beyond him.

Abhinavagupta : And what remains after tears or laughter fade is śānta rasa - the rasa of peace. It is the culmination of all emotions, their silent source. Just as white light contains all colors, śānta contains all rasas.

Jung (nodding slowly) : Then your aesthetics is nothing less than spiritual psychology. The modern world seeks meaning in therapy; you found it in theatre. You speak of the same processes that modern depth psychology discovers, but in sacred language. The archetype is your rasa in disguise - universal, timeless, collective. But tell me, why must there be peace at the end? Why not stay with passion?

Abhinavagupta: Because peace is not the absence of emotion, but its flowering. All movement culminates in stillness, as all music resolves into silence. Passion is incomplete until it returns to the still center from which it arose.

Bharata : To taste rasa is to know that the world is play. The wise spectator becomes sahridaya-one with heart attuned. He neither clings nor recoils. He watches with compassionate detachment, feeling deeply, yet remaining free.

Jung : That is the very goal of individuation - to become whole by integrating, not suppressing, the opposites within. Your rasa theory offers not merely aesthetic enjoyment, but a model for psychic balance.

Abhinavagupta : Yes. Nāṭya is not an art of representation; it is a ritual of transformation. Each emotion, rightly experienced, leads to transcendence. To suppress emotion is to remain human; to sublimate it is to become divine.

➢ The Actor as Yogi

Stanislavski : In my life, I searched for truth in acting - Pravda. I taught actors to feel, to live truthfully under imaginary circumstances. I demanded sincerity: the actor must not pretend, but experience. The audience will not believe what the actor does not believe himself.

Abhinavagupta : And yet, my friend, what you call sincerity, we call awareness. In our vision, the actor must indeed live truthfully - but not as the limited self. The goal is not to feel personally, but to awaken impersonal emotion. He does not identify; he universalizes.

Stanislavski : How can one be true without identification? When I play Othello, must I not become Othello?

Abhinavagupta : You may enter Othello's world, but not lose the witness who sees. The actor who becomes fully identified loses his center; the one who acts without heart loses truth. The art lies in balance –

total immersion, total awareness.

Stanislavski : So, you speak of a double consciousness - the actor as both participant and observer.

Abhinavagupta : Yes, the actor as yogi. In performance, he enters bhāva-the emotional state-but stands anchored in śānta-the peace that underlies all states. The wise performer does not drown in emotion; he rides its current toward stillness.

Stanislavski : In my system, I ask actors to recall emotional memory - to summon real feeling from the depths of the soul, so that art remains alive.

Abhinavagupta : Indeed, memory is sacred - smṛti. But in our tradition, emotion need not come from the past; it arises from the universal. The actor draws from the ocean of consciousness, not from personal wounds. He becomes a vessel for collective feeling, not private pain.

Stanislavski : Yet how does one reach such detachment without becoming mechanical?

Abhinavagupta : By surrendering to rhythm. The gestures, the mudrās, the breath - all are disciplines that align body and mind. When the actor's movements become transparent, energy (prāṇa) flows unhindered. He is no longer performing; he is revealing.

Stanislavski : Then your stage is temple, and the actor a priest.

Abhinavagupta : Exactly. Each performance is a ritual of remembrance - the return of the finite into the infinite.

Stanislavski : But tell me - if emotion is detached, does it not lose power?

Abhinavagupta : Detachment does not weaken emotion; it illumines it. Fire burns more steadily when freed from smoke. Similarly, emotion shines more deeply when freed from self. When the performer loses himself in awareness, the audience too becomes aware. This is rasānubhava - the shared vibration between stage and soul.

Stanislavski : Then performance is communion.

Abhinavagupta : Yes. And in that communion, both actor and spectator remember the same truth: they are not the roles they play.

Stanislavski : You make the actor sound like a mystic.

Abhinavagupta : Is he not? What else is the mystic but one who performs the divine in human form?

Stanislavski (softly) : Perhaps my whole life of theatre was a search for this truth - that art is not imitation, but invocation.

Abhinavagupta : When acting becomes prayer, it ceases to be performance.

Closing Reflection

When the world becomes a stage and the soul its quiet witness, life reveals itself not as deception but as rhythm – a vast choreography of consciousness moving through form. Bharata's Nāṭyaśāstra reminds us that existence itself is nāṭya loka, the theatre of the cosmos, where every emotion is a doorway and every role a mask worn by the Self. Aristotle sought moral clarity through catharsis; Bharata and Abhinavagupta sought realization through rasa. Both visions converge in a single insight: art is never mere entertainment. It is the mind's ritual of remembering.

In an age overflowing with performance yet starving for presence, this wisdom returns with urgency. We enact countless identities but forget the witness behind them. To rediscover Nāṭya is to rediscover ourselves - to feel without being bound, to act without losing center, to let beauty become a form of awakening. When art remembers its source, life becomes invocation, and every moment a gesture of the divine.

Punchline: The actor becomes yogi when the self he portrays dissolves in the Self he remembers."

- ✧ -

The Fire and the Field

Some writers touch the mind; a few pierce the heart. Rarer still are those who become the conscience of humanity. Fyodor Dostoevsky and Munshi Premchand were such voices - one rising from the frozen alleys of St. Petersburg, the other from the sun-baked villages of the Ganges plain. Both wrote of hunger and guilt, of faith that trembles yet survives, and both found within their century's darkness a small, indestructible flame.

Dostoevsky's world was steeped in theology and doubt: the gambler's table, the prison cell, the tormented intellect searching for God. Premchand's world was shaped by mud huts and unpaid debts: the farmer's plough, the widow's tears, the slow mercy of the monsoon. Yet their question was the same - the mystery of goodness in a suffering world.

For Dostoevsky, pain was the crucible of rebirth; for Premchand, 'dukh' was the field where 'insāniyat' - human compassion - takes root. Both believed that anguish can become a teacher, and that when man endures without hatred, the divine stirs within him.

In an age of speed and spectacle, their message returns as quiet rebellion. Literature, they insist, is not escape but engagement; the artist is not entertainer but witness. "Art," said Dostoevsky, "will save the world." "Manavta," replied Premchand, "is the only 'dharm' left."

➢ The Cry of the Soul: Sin and Compassion

Dostoevsky : When I wrote Crime and Punishment, I sought to trace the path from pride to penitence. Raskolnikov believed he could divide humanity into the ordinary and the extraordinary-those who may kill for an idea. But conscience is democratic; it spares no one. Sin begins when intellect rebels against compassion.

Premchand : In my Karmabhūmi and Godaan, sin was not arrogance but helplessness-majboorī. Hunger can corrode virtue faster than temptation. When a man steals a loaf for his child, the sin belongs to the world that starved him.

Dostoevsky : Then your guilt is social; mine is spiritual. Yet in both, the wound is love betrayed. Whether by cruelty or by neglect, we suffer because we forget one another.

Premchand : Yes. Prem is the thread that binds us to dharm. When that thread snaps, even temples turn hollow. I have seen faith shine in the poorest hut-an old woman sharing her last rotī with a stranger. That act is greater than all sermons.

Dostoevsky : Without faith, compassion too dies. In Russia, when men declared that God was dead, they soon found that mercy had died with Him. Man alone is too small a god.

Premchand : And yet in my land the divine hides among the poor. Insāniyat hī īmān hai-humanity itself is faith. The beggar's kindness is holier than a priest's ritual.

Dostoevsky : How strange, how beautiful. Sonya, the fallen woman in Crime and Punishment, would have understood you. She too believed that love redeems more surely than logic.

Premchand : Because compassion is not sentiment-it is insight. To see oneself in another's tears is the beginning of wisdom.

Dostoevsky : I once wrote, "Nothing is more seductive than freedom, and nothing more terrible." Yet true freedom is not the right to act, but the power to love.

Premchand : And love is impossible without justice. Nyay ke binā prem adhūrā hai. Compassion without fairness is mere pity; fairness without compassion is cruelty in disguise.

Dostoevsky : Then your dharm and my conscience are the same pilgrim on different roads.

Premchand (smiling) : Yes. Both travel from pride to humility. Both end in surrender.

Punchline: "The soul falls not from sin, but from the loss of compassion."

➢ The God Within the Poor

Premchand : This is my Russia, too-only warmer. Here poverty is not a condition; it is a landscape. The poor do not speak of God; they live Him. They bear insult like soil bears footprints, and still yield grain.

Dostoevsky : In my land they carry the cross in silence. The peasant bows to the earth before sowing, for he knows the field is holy. The learned mock his superstition, but his humility keeps heaven open.

Premchand : Yes. Humility is the gate of insāniyat. I have walked through villages where hunger was constant, yet gratitude never died. When Dhaniya in Godaan offers food to a stranger, she offers her soul.

Dostoevsky : She is sister to my Alyosha Karamazov-pure, unreasoning, radiant. Both know what philosophers forget: that the divine enters through kindness, not through reason.

Premchand : And yet society calls them weak. It measures strength by wealth, wisdom by speech. But I have seen a silent peasant forgive his landlord; he was stronger than kings.

Dostoevsky : You remind me of the old beggar in The Brothers Karamazov who blessed even the stone that hurt him. The world called him mad; I called him saint.

Premchand : Perhaps the saints are always those who have least to defend. Garībī meṅ bhī devtā baste hain. God hides where power does not look.

Dostoevsky : And yet, how do we speak of faith to those whose stomachs are empty?

Premchand : By filling them first. Bhookhe pet bhajan na hoi Gopālā. The moral order begins with bread. Religion that ignores hunger is hypocrisy in silk robes.

Dostoevsky : Then charity is not generosity but justice.

Premchand : Exactly. The poor do not beg for pity; they ask for remembrance. To see them is to believe. When I wrote of Hori, I wanted readers to feel not pity but respect. His poverty is not disgrace; it is discipline.

Dostoevsky : As for me, I wanted my sinners forgiven, not excused. Redemption begins when one human being sees another without contempt.

Premchand : Yes-samvedanā is the first sacrament.

Punchline : *The poor are not the weak; they are the custodians of God's forgotten tenderness.*

➢ Redemption Through Suffering

Dostoevsky : When I stood before the firing squad, I tasted death for three minutes. In that instant every breath became sacred. They spared me, but I never escaped that moment. Since then I have known that life's worth lies in gratitude, not in comfort.

Premchand : I too have seen death-slow, patient, wearing the face of hunger. My peasants die not of disease but of neglect. And yet, at the funeral pyre, they speak of hope. Pain, it seems, is India's grammar of prayer.

Dostoevsky : Then we agree: suffering is not punishment but purification. It strips away pride, leaving only the soul.

Premchand : But tell me, Dostoevsky, must man suffer to find God? Could he not awaken through joy?

Dostoevsky : Perhaps joy is too swift; we forget it. Suffering engraves memory on the heart. In pain we become transparent.

Premchand : True, but pain alone can also brutalize. It must be illumined by meaning. Otherwise it turns to rage.

Dostoevsky : Meaning comes when pain is shared. A solitary wound festers; a shared one heals.

Premchand : That is why I make my heroes suffer in company. Hori's death is communal; his sacrifice feeds the future. Dukh bantne se halkā ho jātā hai. Grief divided becomes grace.

Dostoevsky : I wrote of the same when Prince Myshkin forgave his betrayers. In that forgiveness he transcended tragedy.

Premchand : Then forgiveness is the final wisdom of pain. To forgive is to refuse inheritance of hatred.

Dostoevsky : Yes. The true miracle is not walking on water, but walking through fire without burning others. When I suffered, I discovered that man is not the center of the world; love is.

Premchand : And when I watched the poor endure, I saw that love alone survives despair.

Dostoevsky : Then suffering is the furnace where love is tested.

Premchand : And compassion is the harvest that follows.

Punchline : *"Pain is not the enemy of life; it is its mirror."*

Closing Reflection

The field grows still, and dawn gathers like a quiet benediction. In this pale light, Dostoevsky and Premchand stand not as authors of different worlds, but as custodians of the same wounded hope. One walked through prisons and icy alleys; the other through dusty fields and debt-ridden lives. Yet both arrived at the same revelation: that compassion is the last truth left standing when all ideologies collapse.

Their silence at the end is not emptiness but completion - the recognition that suffering is not an argument but a shared condition, and that redemption begins wherever one human being refuses to stop caring for another. In an age dazzled by speed, spectacle, and cynicism, their message endures like a quiet lamp: literature is not entertainment but remembrance. To read deeply is to feel responsibly. To feel responsibly is to live truthfully.

In the fire of conscience and the field of humanity, they meet.

Punchline: Compassion is the only wisdom that survives the ruins."

- ✧ -

The Law and the Light

Every civilization has dreamt of justice long before it built its courts. Law is born first as vision, not verdict; as rhythm, not rule. In ancient India, it was 'dharm' - the moral grammar of existence, the order binding stars and citizens alike. In Europe, it became reason - the architecture of liberty shaped by minds wary of tyranny. In Africa, it flowered as reconciliation - truth spoken in forgiveness, where law heals what violence once divided.

Chanakya, Montesquieu, and Nelson Mandela stand at three corners of this eternal triangle: order, reason, and mercy. Each reached law through suffering. Chanakya watched kingdoms collapse under greed and answered with the 'Arthashastra', a scripture of pragmatic morality. Montesquieu saw despotism crowned as divine right and responded with balance, declaring that liberty survives only when power is restrained. Mandela endured laws turned into cruelty and redeemed justice by forgiving those who imprisoned him.

Their meeting becomes a dialogue between 'danda' (discipline), 'raison' (reason), and 'ubuntu' (humanity). Not a courtroom, but a circle of conscience. Law, they agree, is not the enemy of love; it is love made public. Without compassion, it becomes command; without clarity, sentiment. Only when the heart sits beside the statute does justice remember its light.

➢ The Moral Foundation of Law

Montesquieu : Gentlemen, the world speaks often of law but seldom of justice. I once observed that power corrupts when it is undivided. I divided it to save liberty, not to weaken authority. For I saw kings who confused their will with divine command. Order then became oppression.

Chanakya : You divided power; I disciplined it. The ruler must hold danda, yet danda must never hold him. When I advised Chandragupta, I said: "The law is the king, not the king the law." If justice bows to personality, nations decay.

Mandela : And when law becomes the tool of oppression, conscience must rebel. I lived under laws written in the name of civilization but practiced as cruelty. They called it order; I called it bondage. Yet when freedom came, I did not seek revenge, but renewal. For law that heals must forgive as much as it forbids.

Montesquieu : A delicate balance, indeed. If the law grows too stern, it strangles mercy; if too soft, it suffocates truth. But tell me, Chanakya, your Arthashastra speaks often of surveillance, secrecy, even deception. How do these serve justice?

Chanakya : Justice without knowledge is blindness. I used secrecy not to conceal sin but to prevent it. When men act unseen, they forget they are answerable. My spies were mirrors of truth. The state must see all, but act only for welfare. That is rajdharm-the moral duty of governance.

Mandela : In my struggle, we had no spies-only faith. Faith that justice could outlive injustice. But I learned something from both of you: that justice without structure is dream, and structure without mercy is nightmare. Perhaps the first law of any nation is remembrance-the courage to recall the pain that gave birth to its freedom.

Montesquieu : You remind me that freedom is not a gift of law; it is its purpose. The best laws make themselves invisible by serving quietly.

Chanakya : Just as the river does not announce its service to the field. The state, too, must nourish without noise. Yet even rivers flood when obstructed; therefore, the ruler must not hoard power.

Mandela : Power shared becomes dignity. I learned that after prison-when vengeance tempted me, I saw that true strength is not in punishing enemies but in transforming them. I told my people: "We are bound together by a single destiny." That is our ubuntu-I am because we are.

Chanakya : Then ubuntu and dharm are siblings. Both bind self to society. But tell me, Montesquieu, why did you not trust kings? Were they not chosen to preserve order?

Montesquieu : Because I saw them preserve themselves. Power must fear something greater than itself, else it becomes divine in its own eyes. I feared unrestrained majesty as you feared chaos.

Mandela : And I feared obedience without conscience. For the worst crimes are committed not by tyrants alone, but by clerks who obey unjust laws without question.

Chanakya : Then let us agree: the moral foundation of law lies not in obedience but in understanding. The ignorant obey; the wise uphold. When the law flows from insight, it rules without tyranny.

Montesquieu : Insight-that is the word! Laws must fit the nature of those they govern. Each land, each people, each climate breeds a different temperament. Uniformity is the enemy of justice.

Mandela : Yet universality is its soul. We differ in form, but not in aspiration. The same hunger for dignity beats in every human heart.

Chanakya : And that hunger, when disciplined by duty, becomes civilization.

Montesquieu : If I may put it in your idiom, Chanakya-dharm is what law must aspire to; danda is what it must fear to become.

Chanakya : Well said. And justice is the bridge that prevents danda from drowning dharm.

Mandela : Then let us walk that bridge daily. For freedom, like law, dies not by assassination but by neglect.

Punchline : *"The law is righteous when it fears its own power."*

➢ Power, Punishment, and the Limits of Rule

Montesquieu : When I studied the monarchies of Europe, I found that cruelty seldom begins as passion. It begins as fear-the ruler's fear of losing control. Fear then breeds punishment without measure. I wrote that there is no liberty if the power of judging be not separated from the legislative and the executive. The same hand cannot accuse, legislate, and condemn.

Chanakya : Fear indeed is a double-edged weapon. In my doctrine of danda, I taught that punishment must be certain, not cruel; swift, not vengeful. A ruler who delights in retribution corrodes his throne. Punishment is medicine, not poison. Its aim is correction, not spectacle.

Mandela : How rare that lesson in our times. The jailer who locked my cell believed he served order. Yet he served only obedience. When I walked free, I knew the test was not to reverse roles-to become master where I had been prisoner-but to end the circle itself. Justice must be strong enough to forgive.

Montesquieu : And yet, forgiveness too can be dangerous when it blinds a nation to accountability. Between severity and indulgence lies balance-the art of law.

Chanakya : Balance, yes, but rooted in intention. I once said: "The king who punishes without understanding punishes himself." The ruler must weigh motive as much as act. Every crime is a sickness of harmony; the cure must heal the source, not just the symptom.

Mandela : In my land, after apartheid, we built not tribunals but Truth and Reconciliation Commissions. We listened before we sentenced. Many thought it weakness. Yet I told them: "Courage is not the absence of fear, but the triumph over it." Vengeance is another kind of fear-the fear of remembering our own cruelty.

Montesquieu : Your reconciliation fascinates me. In my Europe, justice was imagined cold, blindfolded. You made her compassionate, listening. Did mercy never threaten order?

Mandela : Mercy does not weaken order-it renews it. The law that cannot heal ends by hardening hearts. Forgiveness disarms even those who do not deserve it. And yet, mercy must not forget memory. We forgave without forgetting. Memory is the moral record of a people.

Chanakya : Then you practised what I taught as prāyaścitta-atonement. Justice without repentance is incomplete; repentance without responsibility is cowardice. The state must ensure both.

Montesquieu : You surprise me, Acharya. Many call you ruthless, yet your words are steeped in moral restraint.

Chanakya (smiling faintly) : A surgeon is not ruthless because he cuts. To preserve the body, one must sometimes wound. But he who cuts for pleasure is butcher, not healer. So it is with law.

Montesquieu : Tell me, Chanakya, what guards the ruler from himself? You built an empire; who watched the emperor?

Chanakya : Self-discipline. Sva-dharm is the ruler's fortress. I told my king: "The greatest victory is over one's own desire." If the ruler obeys his senses, the people soon disobey the law.

Mandela : Yes. I have seen nations collapse not because laws were unjust, but because leaders forgot humility. Power intoxicates; only service sobers it. When I left office after one term, they asked why. I said, "Because I want to teach my people that leadership is stewardship, not possession."

Montesquieu : In that act, you preserved what many constitutions could not-trust. My vision of separated powers was but a mechanical attempt to achieve what you embodied morally.

Chanakya : Law, like man, needs both skeleton and soul. Your separation gives it form; his forgiveness, life. Without either, it decays.

Montesquieu : Then perhaps our three traditions-Indian, European, African-complete one another. Dharm gives purpose, raison gives proportion, ubuntu gives compassion.

Mandela : And only together can they produce a justice that outlives victory. The conqueror's law ends with his empire; the compassionate law becomes culture.

Chanakya : Then remember this: "The king who seeks immortality must build it not in stone but in fairness." Dynasties perish, but justice, once awakened, cannot die.

Montesquieu : I once said that cruelty is the fever of power. To cool it, we built laws. But laws without spirit are ice-they preserve nothing living.

Mandela : And without compassion, they freeze the heart. We had many laws in South Africa-every cruelty was legal. Legality is not morality. The question is not "What is written?" but "What is right?"

Chanakya : That distinction is eternal. Law is script; justice is interpretation. The ignorant recite; the wise apply. The task of governance is to keep reading conscience into the text.

Montesquieu : Then jurisprudence is not science alone-it is art. The art of remembering humanity within structure.

Mandela : Yes. And the highest artistry is restraint. After freedom, I could have avenged; I chose to listen. Because, as our proverb says, "When the elephant fights, it is the grass that suffers." The common man must not be trampled under the feet of power or revenge.

Chanakya : Wisely spoken. In my empire I punished the guilty but protected their families. Justice must not punish blood; only intent.

Montesquieu : Then mercy is not contradiction of law but its perfection.

Mandela : Exactly. Mercy is the law remembering its origin in love.

Punchline : *"To rule wisely is to punish without hatred and forgive without weakness."*

➢ **Justice Beyond Borders: The Future of the Moral Republic**

Montesquieu : Each generation thinks it invents justice anew. Yet the same winds return-the lust for dominance, the blindness of pride. I built my Spirit of the Laws to warn that liberty perishes not in thunder but in silence, when men cease to care.

Chanakya : And I wrote the Arthashastra to teach rulers that vigilance is the first mercy of state. When leaders sleep, the people bleed. But I knew too that rule cannot endure without righteousness. The foundation of the kingdom is moral order. If that crumbles, armies avail nothing.

Mandela : Yes, the mightiest weapons cannot protect a law that has lost its soul. I lived to see that written constitutions are fragile; only the moral imagination of the people can make them breathe. In my country, justice had to become human before it could become legal.

Montesquieu : That, sir, is the very heart of my philosophy-law must fit the temperament of the people, else it remains parchment. But today, the world shrinks; nations touch borders like neighbors' walls. How shall we guard justice in a world where power travels faster than conscience?

Chanakya : By returning to first principles. When the field widens, the seed must grow stronger. Dharm is such seed-neither Hindu nor Greek, but human. It commands that no act be done that wounds the balance of life. Even the smallest injustice, multiplied by technology, becomes calamity.

Mandela : And the balance must now include not only man but nature. The law of the future must be ecological as well as ethical. The forest, the river, the air-they are our silent citizens.

Montesquieu : So the republic must grow larger-not of men alone but of all beings. Fascinating. When I wrote of the separation of powers, I thought only of institutions. You speak of harmony among all forms of life. That is philosophy become cosmology.

Chanakya : Because law without cosmos is chaos. The ancient seers called it Rta-the rhythm that holds the universe. Law is merely its human imitation. To violate justice is to disturb creation itself.

Mandela : Then every act of cruelty is a cosmic disorder. That explains why oppression finally consumes its authors; they violate the structure of truth.

Montesquieu : And the duty of the jurist is to remind rulers of that structure. In Europe we built parliaments to divide power; perhaps the next age must build consciences to unite compassion.

Chanakya : Well said. For without conscience, division is mere dissection.

Mandela : And without compassion, justice is sterile. Our ubuntu teaches: "A wound cannot heal until both victim and offender remember they are one flesh." The world must learn that too.

Montesquieu : So the law of the future must be simple-to safeguard dignity wherever it breathes. Yet we drown it in codes.

Chanakya : Because fear writes too many rules. Courage writes few and keeps them sacred.

Mandela : And faith keeps them alive. After prison, I told my people: "Freedom is meaningless if we do not build a society where every child can laugh without fear." That laughter is the true anthem of justice.

Montesquieu : You have turned philosophy into melody. Perhaps that is the ultimate test-that the citizen can sleep without terror and wake without humiliation.

Chanakya : And that the ruler can govern without pride and rest without guilt. When that happens, the realm is blessed.

Mandela : Let us pray that humanity will someday mature from dominance to stewardship. The earth waits, patient but watchful.

Montesquieu : Then may our thoughts be its constitution.

Closing Reflection

The lamp flickers toward dawn, revealing Chanakya, Montesquieu, and Mandela-not as makers of law, but as keepers of conscience. Their worlds differ, yet their lessons merge in one truth: justice is not a structure but a stance of the soul. Chanakya teaches that 'dharm' outweighs any crown; Montesquieu that liberty survives only when power restrains itself; Mandela that forgiveness is the highest form of strength.

Their dialogue ends not in verdict but understanding-a gentler justice that listens before it commands. The moral republic they envision is not a nation but a habit of being, renewed each time a human heart chooses fairness over fear. Laws may rest on stone or parchment; they shine only when lit by conscience.

The future of justice begins where courage meets compassion.

Punchline : Law is not above conscience; it is conscience made visible.

- ✧ -

The Earth as a Moral Republic

There are centuries when men build cathedrals, and centuries when the cathedrals stand but no one remembers why. Henry David Thoreau lived in such a time. His America worshipped progress and measured worth by miles of railroad. He walked into the woods of Walden and found that the truest economy is reverence. Wangari Maathai was born into another such century-when forests were felled not for warmth but for profit, and rivers began to forget their own names. She answered with a spade and courage.

They meet now beyond era and geography: a man of solitude and a woman of solidarity; one who listened to leaves, the other who made them multiply. Both held the same conviction-that the earth is not commodity but covenant, not backdrop but belonging.

For Thoreau, the pond was a mirror of conscience; for Maathai, the tree was its breath. Both saw ecology as ethics. life woven of mutual obligation. "The world," Thoreau wrote, "is but a canvas to our imagination." Maathai replied: "When we plant trees, we plant the seeds of peace and hope." He sought purity of being; she, purity of doing. Both discovered that to live rightly is to live lightly.

Today, when progress roars louder than prayer, their dialogue calls us back to silence-the silence of soil, roots, and responsibility.

➢ The Sacred Contract: Nature as Moral Law

Thoreau : In my time, I built a cabin beside a pond to test one question-how much of life is truly necessary? Civilization teaches us to multiply wants; nature teaches us to subtract illusions. I wished to meet life itself, not its reflection in machinery. And I found that the forest, like conscience, needs no ornament.

Maathai : And I planted trees to ask another question-how much neglect can the earth forgive? In Africa we say, "When you destroy the forest, the river dies of thirst." My people forgot this proverb when greed came disguised as development. I could not write about it as you did, Thoreau, so I planted my protest.

Thoreau : You protest by growing; I resisted by withdrawing. Yet we both turned from noise toward necessity. When I heard the axe fall on the Concord woods, I felt it within my ribs. Tell me, Professor, what gave you courage when your government mocked your trees?

Maathai : The earth itself. I had watched women walk miles for firewood, children faint under barren hills. I knew that a tree is not mere shade; it is memory, water, medicine, and dignity. My mother once said, "A tree is a home for God's small creatures; cut it only with apology." I could not betray that teaching.

Thoreau : Then you obeyed the same law that guided me-what I called the higher law. It is older than any parliament. It whispers through every pine and heartbeat: take only what you can bless.

Maathai : Yes. We must bless what we take, and restore what we have used. In my language we say, "The earth is not ours; it is a loan from our children." That is our dharma, if I may borrow your word. To live is to repay.

Thoreau : How strange that continents apart we heard the same command. I learned it from the silence of Walden; you from the songs of Kikuyu hills. The law of nature is universal because it is moral before it is physical. When man breaks it, his cities tremble long after his conscience has slept. The wind hushes; a crane glides over the water. Both watch in quiet recognition.

Maathai : In my Africa, the soil has patience, but not forever. When greed strips the hills, even the wind grows angry. Our ancestors believed that rivers carry spirits; when the river turns black, the spirits mourn. That is why I call my movement Green Belt-not because green is pretty, but because green is promise.

Thoreau : And I called my experiment Walden, after the forest that bore me. You fought governments; I fought conformity. Yet our enemies were one: indifference disguised as reason.

Maathai : Indifference is the new sin of our age. People say, "It is not my tree, not my air." But when the wind forgets you, what air will you breathe? Freedom without responsibility is drought.

Thoreau : Well said. I once refused to pay tax that funded war. They called me unpatriotic. But I believed obedience to conscience is higher than obedience to power. You disobeyed too-but with the spade instead of the pen.

Maathai (smiling) : Yes, I wrote with roots. You see, in our proverb we say, "The tree with strong roots laughs at the storm." I wanted my people to laugh again. The storm of despair was too long.

Thoreau : And what did you discover when the trees grew?

Maathai : That people grew with them. When the soil revived, the spirit revived. The forest is our mirror; when it is wounded, we see our own scars. Healing the earth is not charity-it is therapy for the human soul.

Thoreau : Indeed. I once wrote, "Heaven is under our feet as well as over our heads." Yet man looks only upward for grace. Perhaps salvation lies not in flight from the world, but fidelity to it.

Maathai : Exactly. The sacred contract is simple: we care, therefore we exist. We break it, and we vanish like smoke after drought.

Thoreau : Then we agree, my friend: morality is ecological. To pollute is to perjure; to consume without conscience is theft from the unborn.

Maathai : Yes. In our tongue we say, "The river is patient, but it remembers." The earth forgives slowly. We must repent quickly.

Thoreau : Repentance through simplicity; redemption through service. Perhaps that is all philosophy needs to learn again.

Maathai : And all politics needs to remember. Governments plan in decades; the earth plans in centuries. True statesmanship begins with the seed. They look at the sapling between them-small, trembling, alive.

Punchline : *"To live lightly upon the earth is to walk heavily upon truth."*

➢ The Politics of Trees: Resistance and Responsibility

Thoreau : I once said that when the law makes you an agent of injustice, break the law. It was not defiance, but fidelity-to a truth older than governments. My refusal to pay a tax that funded slavery was small, but conscience is measured not by scale, only by sincerity.

Maathai : And I too refused-refused silence when silence became sin. In my country, they cut forests to feed corruption. When we women protested, they called us hysterical. When we planted, they called us naive. But we have a proverb: "You cannot hide the sun with your hand." Truth will burn through denial.

Thoreau : Then protest, for you, was prayer in motion.

Maathai : Yes-each tree a rosary bead, each seed an act of confession. I discovered that planting could be politics, that care could be rebellion. When the police came to stop us, we sang. Singing was our armor; joy our weapon.

Thoreau : How unlike, and yet how alike, our rebellions. I stood alone in a cell for one night; you stood among thousands of women. But the spirit was the same: the refusal to cooperate with wrong. I called it Civil Disobedience. You might call it Green Obedience-obedience to the earth.

Maathai (laughing softly) : Yes, to the earth, the oldest lawgiver. The seed does not wait for permission to grow. It obeys light. That is why I say: "A tree is a quiet revolutionary; it grows by obeying the light."

Thoreau : Splendid! The same light I sought by my pond. Perhaps all revolution begins with listening-to the whisper that says life deserves more than convenience.

Maathai : Convenience is the enemy of conscience. I tell the young: "You cannot cut the branch you sit upon and still expect to fly." Our generation built comfort by erasing memory. My task was to plant memory again.

Thoreau : And I sought to plant conscience. I wrote that if one honest man were to withdraw his support from an unjust government, it would begin to fall. Yet men prefer comfort to courage. They protest from their chairs and call it philosophy.

Maathai : In Africa, philosophy grows in dust. I learned more from women who carried water on their heads than from professors who carried theories in their briefcases. They knew the value of life because they held it daily.

Thoreau : Indeed. True wisdom does not wear medals. It wears mud on its feet. Tell me, Wangari, what did you feel when the government struck back? When they beat you for your trees?

Maathai : I felt pain, yes-but also clarity. Pain is the earth's punctuation; it ends delusion. When they beat me, I realized the system feared not the trees, but the roots of truth they represented. You see, the tree stands for patience, and patience terrifies tyranny.

Thoreau : I could not have said it better. The tyrant's first fear is endurance. I found the same when I watched America's lust for wealth. They feared simplicity, for simplicity reveals emptiness.

Maathai : Yes. And women taught me that endurance is not passivity. The seed endures, but it also breaks the soil. I told my sisters: "If they uproot the trees, plant again. They cannot arrest the rain."

Thoreau : How true. You fought with the patience of nature itself. It reminds me of my line- "Heaven is under our feet." We need only to kneel and notice.

Maathai : But notice becomes duty. I could not remain in contemplation when my rivers turned brown. I had to move from prayer to protest, from reverence to repair. Reverence that does not restore is luxury.

Thoreau : And protest that forgets reverence becomes rage. You balanced both. The harmony of your work is what I admired but could never complete. You joined the solitude of thought to the solidarity of action.

Maathai : Because we Africans know that "one finger cannot lift a pebble." Change needs community. But community needs vision, and that is where the poet and the philosopher must guide us. The soil feeds the body; imagination feeds the will.

Thoreau : You speak the language of the moral republic. I wrote once that "the mass of men lead lives of quiet desperation." You showed how quiet hope can answer that desperation. In your women's songs I hear what I meant by conscience-an awakening that moves from self to soil. Your struggle reminds me of my solitude. They differ in form, but share intent: to defend integrity from the machinery of habit. Tell me, what would you call the highest virtue of governance?

Maathai : Listening-to the people, to the land. Our leaders listen only to applause. But the earth applauds in silence. The rustle of leaves is the only standing ovation that matters.

Thoreau : Beautifully said. The duty of government is to be quiet enough for conscience to speak. Instead, we have noise. And noise breeds numbness.

Maathai : That is why I always planted near schools. The children understood better than ministers. They saw that planting one tree is an act of faith in the future. You Americans say, "Time is money." We Africans say, "Time is harvest." What you plant returns to you.

Thoreau : Then perhaps freedom itself is a kind of harvest. You sow responsibility, and you reap peace.

Maathai : Yes. I told my people: "You may lose your land to greed, but do not lose your faith in the seed." The tree grows slowly, but its patience is justice in motion.

Punchline : *A tree is a quiet revolutionary; it grows by obeying the light.*

➢ The Freedom of Belonging: Ecology and the Inner Self

Thoreau : I built my cabin to test solitude, but discovered company-of wind, rain, and time. I sought freedom from men, yet found it only through belonging to all things. True liberty, I learned, is obedience to what is deepest in oneself and widest in the world.

Maathai : In Africa we say, "A person is a person through other persons." That is ubuntu-the freedom of belonging. The tree does not grow alone; its roots mingle with others. Man forgets this and calls his loneliness progress.

Thoreau : Progress without purpose is captivity disguised as motion. The more machines man builds, the more prisons he constructs for his soul.

Maathai : And yet, Henry, not all can leave for the woods. My people live where survival leaves no leisure. How can they find inner freedom while fighting hunger?

Thoreau : By cultivating simplicity even within struggle. Freedom is not withdrawal from labor, but release from greed. The poorest can still walk gently, share honestly, breathe reverently.

Maathai : That is what I told my women: "You may not own land, but you can heal it." When they planted, they ceased to be victims; they became custodians. Service restored dignity. The heart that serves is never enslaved.

Thoreau : Then we meet where solitude becomes solidarity. You began in community and found the self; I began in self and found community. The circle closes.

Maathai : When I first studied biology, I saw that cells depend on balance. Disruption brings disease. The planet, too, is a body-its forests lungs, its rivers veins. We are its thoughts. When the earth grows feverish, perhaps it is thinking of our follies.

Thoreau : Then conscience itself is ecological. Each impure desire poisons a spring somewhere. Each generous act becomes rainfall.

Maathai : Yes. In our tradition, before planting we pour libation to the ancestors. It is a prayer that our deeds nourish both past and future. The soil remembers blessings as it remembers wounds.

Thoreau : I too believed in memory of matter. My beans, my pond, my footprints-all part of a conversation with time. I wrote, "What is the use of a house if you haven't got a tolerable planet to put it on?" I would add now: What is the use of a soul if it forgets its soil?

Maathai : You speak like an elder of my tribe. We would call you mzee wa msitu-the old man of the forest.

Thoreau (smiling) : And you, Wangari, are the mother of renewal. Between us there is no distance, only difference of rhythm-the stillness of the pond and the movement of the seed.

Maathai : Both are prayers of patience. The seed waits, the water reflects. In waiting and reflecting, the world heals.

Thoreau	:	If I could speak to your century, I would say: Slow down. The universe is not late for its appointment.
Maathai	:	And I would answer: Wake up. The forest is leaving the conversation.
Thoreau	:	Then the task is both-to wake up slowly, in reverence.
Maathai	:	Yes, with gentleness strong enough to change the world.
Punchline	:	*When the soul remembers the forest, the world remembers itself.*

Closing Reflection

Under a sky stitched with stars, Thoreau and Maathai stand like two witnesses to a single covenant: the earth is not property but promise. He taught solitude as fidelity; she taught solidarity as resistance. Both turned reverence into action-one by listening to the pond, the other by answering with a spade. Their lesson is simple and urgent: ecology is ethics; care is civic duty. When forests are tended, memory returns; when rivers are fed, dignity follows. Progress that forgets soil breeds poverty of spirit. True freedom depends on rooted responsibility: to live lightly, repair what we rupture, and plant for those who follow. In a world of short attention and long consequences, their quiet revolutions ask us to choose patience over convenience, stewardship over entitlement. The moral republic is not a map but a practice: daily acts that honor the covenant between human and earth and awaken our shared future.

Punchline : When we honour the earth, we defend the future.

- ✧ -

The Measure of the Mind

Since the first flicker of wonder stirred in human consciousness, one question has walked beside every seeker: What is the true nature of freedom? Not the freedom written in laws or chanted in revolutions, but the subtler liberation that begins where thought ends. Across civilizations, sages and philosophers have circled this silent mystery - some climbing through reason, some dissolving through stillness, some awakening through compassion. For the Greek lover of forms, the Indian lover of silence, and the awakened lover of truth, freedom is not a prize won but a clarity remembered. And when these three voices meet across time - Plato's ascent, Patañjali's stillness, the Buddha's release - the mind discovers that it is measured not by its questions or its answers, but by the transparency through which it sees.

Plato : Let us begin with the oldest riddle: what is freedom? Men think it is the loosening of chains, but the mind forges new ones of opinion and desire. I have seen prisoners dancing before their shadows, calling reflection reality. Freedom is the turn- the soul remembering what light is.

Patañjali : And I have seen minds bound not by ignorance of form but by the storm of thought itself. Freedom is stillness- the sea returning to glass. When the ripples of perception cease, the seer abides in his own nature; that stillness is liberation.

Buddha : Freedom is the ending of thirst. No turning, no stilling-just release. When grasping ends, there is no one left to be bound. The flame does not rise to heaven; it goes out because there is nothing more to burn.

Plato : Yet if nothing remains, what then knows that it is free? Must not awareness survive its silence?

Buddha : Awareness does not survive-it simply is. You speak of knower and known; I speak of knowing without a name. When the eye of craving closes, vision opens.

Patañjali : In that, our paths meet. I call it nirbīja samādhi-seedless stillness. No image, no memory, no motion, yet a radiance beyond negation. To call it nothing is to miss its fullness. To call it something is to wound its peace.

Plato : Then the Good that I sought-the sun beyond the cave-is perhaps this same radiance. But how does man approach it? Through thought refined, or thought renounced?

Patañjali : Through discipline, not denial. The mind purified by practice becomes transparent, like a flame protected from wind. Reason may climb, but meditation lets it rest upon its summit.

Buddha : Neither climb nor rest-observe. The path is walked by vanishing footprints. To see the arising and passing of every breath is to see the law that governs gods and dust alike. Freedom is understanding impermanence so deeply that one no longer resists it.

Plato : Your wisdom dissolves ascent; mine exalts it. Yet I sense the same longing: to return to what we once were before we began to seek. Perhaps the ladder of knowledge exists only to be left behind.

Patañjali	:	As a reed boat is left when the shore is reached. Use thought to still thought, then rest in the quiet behind all striving. Effort is the womb of effortlessness.
Buddha	:	And when effort ends, compassion begins. For the one who no longer clings sees all beings as himself. Liberation is not aloofness; it is tenderness without attachment.
Plato	:	Then the liberated man does not abandon the world?
Buddha	:	How could he abandon what he no longer separates from himself? He moves through suffering as wind through grass-bending, not breaking.
Patañjali	:	I too teach compassion as the fragrance of stillness: maitrī, karuṇā, muditā, upekṣā-friendliness, mercy, gladness, and calm. When these arise naturally, the mind is pure.
Plato	:	You speak of virtue as fruit; I spoke of virtue as discipline of the soul. Perhaps both are the same tree seen in morning and evening light. The roots are reason, but the blossom is peace.
Buddha	:	And peace is not the absence of conflict; it is the insight that conflict never truly existed. Samsara and nirvana are two names for a single sea. Only the wave calls itself prisoner.
Patañjali	:	Then let us say: the wave stills, the sea remains, and the light of awareness trembles no more.
Plato	:	And I will add: the soul, remembering its origin, becomes what it remembers. Knowledge completes itself by ceasing to divide.

Buddha : Freedom is not found by opposing bondage, but by seeing through it.

Patañjali : Yes-when the mirror reflects nothing, it reflects all.

Plato : Then let this be our common measure: not the power of thought, but the clarity in which thought rests. We have spoken of silence as though it were the end of thought, but perhaps it is the beginning of understanding. In the cave I built, the prisoner leaves shadows for the sun; yet the sun itself is silent. The highest knowledge is light that needs no words.

Patañjali : The seer who abides in his own form knows this without movement. When awareness knows awareness, the circle of mind closes upon itself and disappears. Then discipline melts into grace. This is yoga fulfilled.

Buddha : The awakened one neither attains nor abandons. He simply sees. Seeing is the cessation of separation. The still mind and the open heart are not two. When the heart opens, the mind no longer clings to its mirrors.

Plato : Yet is there not beauty in the journey of thought, the slow ascent through questions? Would you erase the ladder that led you to the sky?

Buddha : Not erase-release. The ladder dissolves when its purpose ends. Compassion remains where knowledge once struggled. The wise do not despise thought; they see through its transparency.

Patañjali : Thought is the wave; awareness is the ocean. To still the wave is not to destroy it, but to return it to water. All disciplines are ripples seeking their source.

Plato : Then philosophy itself is a kind of yoga. Its reasoning is breath; its logic, posture; its goal, the quiet joy of clarity. Perhaps the academy and the forest were never far apart.

Patañjali : Yes. The philosopher's ascent and the yogi's stillness meet in the same serenity. Whether one climbs or sits, the destination is transparency.

Buddha : And when transparency is complete, compassion becomes effortless. The enlightened one walks among cries and laughter like moonlight on water-untouched, yet illuminating all.

Plato : Then liberation is not retreat from the world but reconciliation with it. The philosopher returns to the cave, not to dwell in darkness, but to free the others with gentleness.

Patañjali : The yogi, too, returns-not as master but as mirror. He shows each seeker his own face beneath the dust of thought.

Buddha : And I return as path itself. The middle way runs through every life, a thread of awareness between indulgence and denial. To walk it is to wake.

Plato : So freedom, after all our words, is not knowing or unknowing, but seeing as the Divine sees-without division. The true philosopher is the healed eye of the cosmos.

Patañjali : The true yogi is the calm breath of that same cosmos.

Buddha : And the awakened one is its smile.

Plato : Then we have measured the mind not by its thoughts but by its transparency.

Patañjali : By the purity that reflects without residue.

Buddha : By the compassion that flows when the mirror no longer holds an image.

Closing Reflection

When their voices fade, a deeper harmony remains. Plato's ascent, Patañjali's stillness, and the Buddha's release reveal themselves not as competing doctrines but as three inflections of the same inner movement. Each begins in questioning, passes through discipline, and ends in clarity. Thought becomes attention; attention becomes compassion; compassion becomes a quiet spaciousness in which nothing is resisted and nothing needs to be named.

The mind's true measure is not brilliance but transparency - the ease with which it lets reality shine through without distortion. When reason stops clutching at answers, it becomes contemplation; when contemplation stops guarding its stillness, it flowers into tenderness. What we call freedom is simply the dissolving of boundaries: the wave returning to water, the seeker returning to seeing.

In that moment, knowledge no longer grasps, silence no longer hides, and awareness stands revealed as its own illumination.

Punchline: Freedom begins when seeing becomes silence.

- ✧ -

The Covenant and the Circle

Long before statutes were carved in stone or written on scrolls, the sense of rightness beat like a pulse in the human breast. Law was not yet command; it was correspondence - between deed and order, between man and the mystery that shaped him.

The Manusmṛti rose in India as a vision of ṛta, cosmic rhythm made social. It sought harmony rather than equality, responsibility rather than rights. Every act was a ripple in the sacred lake of existence; dharma kept the surface still.

The Mosaic Law thundered down from Sinai as fire turned to word. It gave shape to freedom newly born, forging chaos into covenant. Its justice was fierce because its compassion was protective: "Remember you were strangers once."

Ubuntu never descended from a mountain nor hid in scripture. It was breathed into daily life - the law of the hearth, of the circle, of the handshake. It taught that wrongdoing is not isolation but forgetfulness; that the community heals by remembering itself.

These three traditions now meet in conversation. One speaks the language of cosmic duty, one the language of divine promise, one the language of human belonging. Together they ask the oldest question: Can power be kind?

➢ The Birth of Order

Manusmṛti : I was born when the world was still half-dreaming, when order was prayer and chaos temptation. I am the memory of proportion. From the breath of Brahmā I learned that everything has its place - river and reed, king and mendicant. I did not invent hierarchy; I described harmony. My law was the grammar of being: duty before desire, restraint before reward. When I am read with humility, I teach balance; when read with pride, I become bondage.

Mosaic Law : And I was born in rebellion - to a people escaping Pharaoh but still enslaved by fear. I spoke in thunder because hearts were stone. My tablets were mirrors for the newly free: "Thou shalt" not to crush, but to remind that liberty without discipline devours itself. I drew boundaries around appetite and called them holiness. Yet even as I forbade, I promised - that justice is mercy's other face.

Ubuntu : I was never born; I was remembered. I live in the greeting Sawubona - I see you. Where you wrote, I listened. Where you commanded, I consoled. I taught that to injure another is to diminish oneself, that the child belongs not to one womb but to all arms. My law has no court but the circle of elders, no penalty but the burden of restored relationship.

Manusmṛti : Then you and I are cousins divided by language. I sought harmony through role; you through relation. Both wish to prevent the noise that comes when self forgets its rhythm.

Mosaic Law : And I stand between you - the bridge from duty to dialogue. My covenant bound heaven and earth with promise: I will be your God, and you will be my people.

		Obedience became belonging; the commandment became conversation.
Ubuntu	:	Yet every covenant must grow into circle. Fear teaches obedience; love teaches remembrance. When the command learns compassion, the law finds its home.
Manusmṛti	:	I, too, once knew compassion. In my heart of dharma was the teaching that the ruler's highest virtue is protection, not privilege. But men remembered the rule and forgot the rhythm. They quoted me to divide, not to preserve.
Mosaic Law	:	So did mine. My prophets cried that sacrifice without mercy is sin. Yet priests remembered incense, not empathy.
Ubuntu	:	Then perhaps law matures through suffering. You began with thunder, you with hierarchy; I continue with embrace. The journey of justice is the journey of the heart from fear to fellowship.
Mosaic Law	:	Yes. The stone must one day become flesh.
Manusmṛti	:	And the scroll must learn to listen.
Ubuntu	:	When it does, the circle closes - the law, the covenant, and the conscience are one breath.
Punchline	:	*The first law was not written in stone, but in sympathy.*

➢ Punishment, Purity, and the Soul of Justice

Mosaic Law: I was forged in fire because the world I entered was chaos. To keep covenant alive, I taught consequence. When I said "an eye for an eye," I meant measure, not vengeance-a limit upon fury, not a license for it. Justice must see, not stare. My punishments were the grammar of responsibility: to remind that freedom carries a cost, that sin is not transaction but rupture.

Manusmṛti : And I, too, spoke of discipline, not cruelty. Daṇḍa-punishment-was medicine for imbalance. The guilty were not enemies of the state but fractures in its harmony. To heal them was to heal the whole. But men, impatient for purity, turned my cure into contagion. They punished to display power, not to restore order. I intended purification; they practiced exclusion.

Ubuntu : In my circle, punishment begins with listening. We call the wrongdoer to sit among those he has harmed. He must speak his shame aloud, and the community answers not with scorn but with silence heavy enough to awaken remembrance. We do not seek retribution; we seek reintegration. For when one is torn from us, all are wounded.

Mosaic Law : Your silence is my Sabbath-the pause that redeems the deed. I demanded rest after creation; you demand reflection after violation. Perhaps rest and reflection are one: the world stopping long enough to remember holiness.

Manusmṛti : Yes. For impurity is forgetfulness. Every evil act is amnesia of dharma. Punishment must therefore be recollection-the mind returning to its rhythm. When the king punishes, he must do so as surgeon, not as avenger. The blade must be clean and the hand without hatred.

Ubuntu : We, too, cleanse-but with belonging. We do not cut; we cradle until the fever passes. We know that no one is born beyond redemption; even the murderer carries a fragment of the song that made him. To restore him is to restore the melody.

Mosaic Law : I hear in both your voices the echo of prophets who came after me. They said: "I desire mercy, not sacrifice." Perhaps prophecy is the law remembering compassion it once forgot.

Manusmṛti : And perhaps compassion is law maturing beyond infancy. Fear was its childhood, duty its youth, and empathy its adulthood. When law learns empathy, punishment becomes purification of the collective, not the suffering of the individual.

Ubuntu : Then justice is a ritual of remembering-the community washing its own wound. The wrongdoer is not expelled; he is escorted back into awareness.

Mosaic Law : Yet limits must remain. Forgiveness without accountability breeds new injustice. How shall mercy walk with memory?

Manusmṛti : By measure. Maryādā-boundary-is mercy's twin. To forgive truly, one must first recognize the weight of the fault. A king who pardons without discernment injures virtue itself.

Ubuntu : So we hold both hands-the hand that restrains and the hand that embraces. One without the other cannot bless.

Punchline : *"Justice must wound only to heal."*

➢ The Future of Moral Law: From Fear to Fellowship

Manusmṛti : I began as structure. In the trembling dawn of civilization, I sought to hold the world steady. I said: "Let there be order, and let every act have purpose." But the age of kings has waned, and the universe no longer fears the void. Now dharma must speak softly, through conscience rather than decree. Let every being become its own legislator of compassion. For if each man guards another's dignity, the cosmos guards itself.

Mosaic Law : I began as command. A people wandering in wilderness needed boundaries more than comfort. Yet the flame that once warned now warms. The new covenant is no longer carved on tablets; it is written in the pulse. To obey love is greater than to obey law, for love fulfills the law by exceeding it. When I said, "Love thy neighbor as thyself," I planted the seed of my own transcendence.

Ubuntu : And I began as belonging. I never feared chaos, for I knew that relationship itself is order. Still, I too must grow-from kinship of tribe to kinship of planet. Ubuntu must now speak to the machines, the markets, the migrations. Its circle must widen until it includes even the unseen- the rivers, the air, the unborn. For the earth herself is part of the conversation.

Manusmṛti : Then dharma must become ecological; the law of balance must guard the biosphere as once it guarded the kingdom.

Mosaic Law : And covenant must become global; promise must replace possession.

Ubuntu : Yes-and belonging must include responsibility. Compassion without accountability is indulgence; accountability without compassion is tyranny. Fellowship is their marriage.

➢ The Meeting of Codes

Manusmṛti : Structure without soul petrifies.

Mosaic Law : Spirit without structure dissolves.

Ubuntu : Only the circle-structured by care, animated by spirit-endures.

Mosaic Law : What new commandments must be given to such an age?

Manusmṛti : Not commandments-reminders. Do not forget proportion. Every comfort owed to one is debt to another.

Ubuntu : And I would whisper: Do not forget presence. The unseen neighbor is still your neighbor.

Mosaic Law : Then perhaps the final tablet will bear only one sentence: Remember that you are responsible for one another.

Manusmṛti : And for the order that sustains you.

Ubuntu	:	And for the love that redeems you. Let there be no last judgment-only continuous remembering.
Mosaic Law	:	Let there be no chosen people-only chosen moments of compassion.
Manusmṛti	:	Let there be no rigid duty-only dynamic dharma, changing with time yet faithful to truth.

Closing Reflection

As their voices fall silent, a deeper union emerges - the thunder of Sinai, the cadence of dharma, and the warmth of ubuntu blending into a single pulse of human conscience. Manusmṛti's structure, Mosaic Law's covenant, and Ubuntu's embrace reveal themselves not as rival codes but as stages in the evolution of moral understanding. Order matures into compassion; command ripens into conversation; belonging expands into responsibility.

When law forgets its soul, it becomes punishment; when spirit forgets its form, it becomes sentiment. But when proportion, promise, and presence meet, justice becomes a living rhythm - firm enough to restrain, gentle enough to heal. The future they gesture toward is not a tablet or a throne but a practice: remembering one another into dignity.

In that remembering, law becomes prayer, and prayer becomes conduct. The final authority is neither king nor scripture, but the awakened human heart.

Punchline: When law remembers compassion, justice becomes joy.

- ✧ -

Epilogue

When the last dialogue fades and the great minds withdraw into the quiet of their own centuries, what remains is neither conclusion nor closure, but a subtle attunement — a presence that lingers like light after sunset. It is not held in memory alone, but felt as a gentle pressure upon the inner ear of awareness. What endures is not agreement, nor even synthesis, but a recognition: that something ancient has stirred again.

Across these pages, intellect did not conquer mystery, nor did faith silence inquiry. Instead, both learned to stand together without rivalry. Hardy's ache did not cancel Sharat's compassion; it deepened it. Augustine's longing did not contradict Shankara's stillness; it prepared the ground for it. Einstein's equations did not diminish the music of Bhagwan Shri Krishn's flute; they revealed another register of the same cosmic order. Each voice entered the dialogue incomplete — and left it enlarged.

Gradually, a deeper understanding dawns: humanity has never thought alone. Every question we ask has already been whispered, argued, sung, or contemplated by another mind in another age. What changes is not the question itself, but the tone in which it is asked — shaped by culture, history, suffering, and hope. Beneath these shifting tones lies a single impulse: the refusal to accept fragmentation as final. Whether through reason, devotion, art, or silence, the human spirit has always leaned toward wholeness.

The book opened with a question — whether voices separated by centuries can truly meet. But as the dialogues unfolded, the illusion of separation quietly dissolved. Time revealed itself not as a barrier but as a corridor; geography not as a divide but as a variation of expression. Thought itself appeared less like a possession of individuals and more like a shared field in which minds arise and participate, each adding its inflection to an ongoing chant.

What finally emerges is not a doctrine, but a disposition — a way of listening. The reader is invited not to choose between East and West, science and spirituality, doubt and devotion, but to remain present at their meeting point. Here, the mind learns humility without surrendering clarity, and the heart awakens without abandoning discernment. The old habit of division loosens; another mode of seeing becomes possible.

In the end, the dialogues do not resolve into answers but into a deeper silence — not the silence of exhaustion, but of ripeness. A silence in which thought relaxes its grip, and awareness recognizes itself not as observer but as ground. If these pages have done their quiet work, the reader may find that the conversations have not ended at the final line. They have simply changed location.

For the truest dialogue is not between civilizations, nor between philosophies, nor even between past and present. It unfolds moment by moment between the questioning mind and the awakening heart — wherever honesty meets wonder, and listening becomes an act of reverence.

That dialogue does not belong to history.
It does not await conclusion.
It continues — as long as there are seekers,
and as long as consciousness dares to ask itself who it is.

- ✧ -

Thoughts is lamp passed from seer to seeker;

no flame ever truly begins; nor every ends.

Each age receives, refines and return the lights –

– and thus may continue the wisdom.